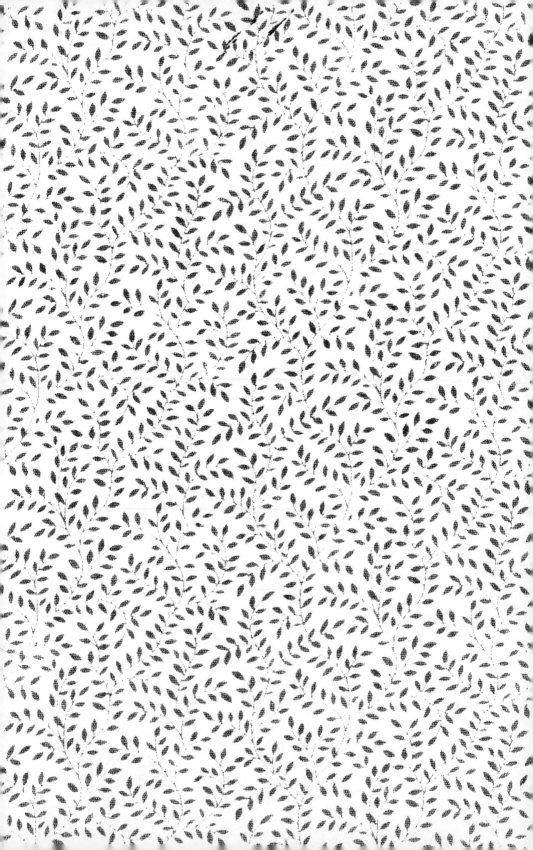

Forget Me Not

Forget Me Not

Caring for and Coping with Your Aging Parents

Alan P. Siegal, M.D.
Robert S. Siegal

Celestial Arts
Berkeley, California

The tables appearing on pages 149–155: Expectation of Life, United States, 1979–81 to 1992; Expectation of Life at Selected Ages, by Race and Sex, United States, 1990–02 to 1991; Expectation of Life Rates at Single Years of Age by Race and Sex; Expectation of Mortality Rates at Single Years by Race and Sex; are used with the gracious cooperation of Metropolitan Life Insurance Company.

Cover design by Fifth Street Design
Text design by Sarah Levin

FIRST CELESTIAL ARTS PRINTING 1993

Library of Congress Cataloging-in-Publication Data
Siegal, Alan P.
    Forget me not : caring for and coping with your
aging parents / by Alan P. Siegal and Robert Siegal.
        p.   cm. $9.95
    ISBN 0-89087-691-6 : $9.95
    1. Aging parents—Care—United States.
    2. Aging parents—Health and hygiene—United States.
    3. Aged—Services for—United States.   4. Aging
parents—United States—Family relationships.
    I. Siegal, Robert.   II. Title.
    HV1461.S535   1993   93-403
    362.6'0973—dc20   CIP

1 2 3 4 5 6 7 8 / 99 98 97 96 95 94 93

Contents

This book is dedicated to our parents,
Evelyne and Murray Siegal; to Evelyn, Jessica,
Melissa, and Max for their love and support;
to Robin, Lauren, Marcy, Alexander, and Brian with
love and thanks; to the patients and their families for the
privilege of sharing their lives and their stories with us;
to Cassie Pollack for her overwhelming contribution;
to Barbara Hogenson for faith and encouragement;
and to our editors,
Colleen Paretty and Veronica Randall
for making this book a reality.

Introduction

When you get right down to it, life just isn't fair. If it were, we would all age in perfect health, spend time with those we love, and participate in all the activities we enjoy until our final day arrived. Then we'd kiss our loved ones, bid everyone farewell, and simply lay down to sleep and not wake up the next morning.

Yet life is seldom this accommodating. Though people are living longer than ever before, this longevity is often accompanied by increased frailty, loss of mental faculties, or other problems that require long-term medical care. Increasingly, that care is either supplied by health care professionals or managed by the adult children of those requiring this care.

But there is a tremendous lack of adequate training to prepare adult children for the role of caregiver. This unpreparedness does not, however, absolve them of responsibility for their elderly parents. Nevertheless, being forced to suddenly face the prospect of providing care for a parent can be an emotionally and physically overwhelming task.

If you're reading this book, it means one of several things: Your parent has just suffered a medical catastrophe and you're trying to handle the situation; or, you've noticed that your parent's mental or physical condition seems to be degenerating and you're unsure of what to do; or, you have the foresight to realize that while you don't need the information in this book today, at some point you will and are wisely planning for that time.

If you are in the midst of a crisis, you will undoubtedly learn from this experience and appreciate the value of some advance planning. As soon as the current situation is stabilized, you can apply the lessons you've learned for the benefit of other elderly parents and relatives you may need to care for one day.

Unfortunately, many people assume that years of training and study are required to care for their elderly parent or relative. But in fact the most important qualification is simply the willingness to care. If you have the desire to do what's necessary, you can do what is necessary. That said, you should understand it is our belief that, as with most things in life, the so-called Golden Rule or Me Rule, as we refer to it, applies unequivocally to every aspect of caregiving. All you need to do is keep in mind at every turn how you would like to be treated in a similar situation, and act accordingly. What goes around truly comes around.

But the purpose of this book is not to instill guilt, nor do we suggest that it is the obligation of every child to care for his or her parent in their home as opposed to other alternatives. For many people, logistical, lifestyle, emotional, or financial considerations simply make such an arrangement impossible. However, you and your siblings and other family members, if appropriate, are expected to make a direct impact on the care your parent receives. The purpose of this book is to give you the tools you need to make intelligent, informed decisions on your parent's behalf, and to cope with the emotional and financial consequences of these actions.

These pages are divided into three parts: Caring, Coping, and Resources.

Part One addresses a variety of practical approaches one can take to manage medical crises, as well as how to put a plan of care together for an aging parent. It is not meant to replace the advice of doctors, nurses, or social workers. Rather, its intention is to provide you with an overview of health care services that you can tap into specifically for the care of your parent. Also, we address Medicare and Medicaid regulations as well as a number of legal documents and financial considerations that can help make your job as a caregiver easier.

Part Two discusses ways to manage the emotional burdens that caregiving can place on you, specifically with your parents, spouse, siblings, children, and employer. We also devote a chapter to you—how to help yourself and seek professional assistance if necessary.

Part Three is a resource section with the names, addresses, and phone numbers of all fifty state agencies on aging, along with a listing of many national organizations related to eldercare, as well as some sample documents and suggested reading.

Our hope is that this book's information will provide practical advice, useful information, and immediate guidance to help you better manage your role as a caregiver. We encourage you to share this book with friends and loved ones who are faced with—or may one day face—similar situations.

Good luck.

Part I

Caring

Chapter 1

When the Call Comes

*S*ally *is forty-nine years old, married, and an administrative assistant for a vice president of a Fortune 500 company. She called our office one day asking for help with her mother, seventy-three, who had hip-replacement surgery five days earlier and was about to be discharged from the hospital.*

The doctor told Sally that her mom needs acute rehabilitation (a physical therapy regimen, designed to restore the body's normal level of functioning following surgery, in a rehabilitation center or nursing home) and that discharging her to her home is out of the question. In addition to the hip fracture, the doctor is concerned that Sally's mother also suffers from mental lapses (such as short-term memory loss, difficulty with problem solving, and so on) consistent with a diagnosis of dementia.

Sally, who has spent the last five days at her mother's bedside is totally unprepared to deal with this situation. Her mother lives with her sister in a private home on Long Island. Sally lives with her husband and two children in Connecticut. She has no idea what to do.

We considered the details of Sally's problem, and recommended that her mother undergo rehabilitation at a nursing home in Connecticut, close to her daughter's home, so that Sally could monitor the situation. Shortly after her mother was transferred to the nursing home, arrangements were made for an assessment of the dementia problems that worried her doctor. As rehabilitation progressed, this appeared to be less of an issue. Rather, the analgesics and medications used to control pain after the hip surgery probably added to an acute delirium noted by the doctor in the hospital.

After a four-week rehabilitation in the nursing home, Sally's mother was transferred to her daughter's home for another six weeks of home-health assistance (skilled nursing and other health care provided at home) and physical therapy. Later, the mother returned to her own home with her sister.

Yes, caring is hard

You've made a conscious effort to care, and you should be commended. Caring takes work; it takes a physical and emotional effort. Certainly, it is easier to pass the buck or simply look the other way. And while you may never get the "thank you" that you deserve, know in your heart that your efforts are making a difference and are appreciated.

Few experiences are as devastating as receiving a call in the middle of the night telling you that an accident or illness has necessitated the hospitalization of a loved one, especially a parent. Your first thought, naturally, is to do something, anything. But what? Call your siblings? Jump in the car and race to the hospital? Pack a bag and run to the airport? Call your parent's physician? Your physician? Your next steps will likely be dictated by a combination of factors: your parent's condition, your proximity to your parent, and your own family and work requirements.

Like so much else in life today, recent changes in society impact your specific situation. Before America became a mobile society, families often lived near one another. Parents either lived with their children in the same home, or on their own but in the same community. Most men worked while women stayed home to care for children and tend to domestic chores, and were more readily available when family crises arose.

Times, of course, are very different. More than half the women in America work outside the home. Siblings and parents often live in different towns or states. Responding to health care crises now requires significant planning, coordination, and sacrifice. And, most often, women still bear the responsibility for managing these crises. Statistics show that 60 percent of the caregivers for the elderly are the elderly themselves, spouses mostly. Approximately 30 percent are daughters and daughters-in-law, and the remaining 10 percent are sons and sons-in-law. While traditional roles have changed somewhat, traditional responsibilities have not.

Even if there is another parent around to help, the burden often falls to the daughter (or daughter-in-law) who lives nearest—but this can be a highly subjective issue. Let's say mom and dad are in Dallas, the daughter is in

New York, and the son is in Los Angeles. It is not unusual for the daughter to drop everything and hop on a plane. Why? He argues that his career is more important than her career, her life is more flexible than his. And, of course, issues of guilt often inflame the whole discussion. Many times it's simply the guilt, and not always the acuteness of the situation, that puts either sibling on the plane. We'll deal with guilt and other emotional issues in Part Two: Coping.

Health care is different

Just as lifestyles have changed, health care has changed. The traditional family doctor, who took care of everyone from birth to death and could be depended on to handle any situation, has given way to the age of the specialist. The role of the community hospital, which was the source of ongoing medical care beyond acute-care treatment (immediate treatment, such as surgery, needed during the most serious phase of an illness), where a patient would remain after surgery for several weeks for rehabilitation before returning home, has also changed dramatically.

Now, because of the system of supervising care and making payments that is used by Medicare, that scenario doesn't exist. Today, hospitals use DRGs (diagnostic-related groups), in which payment for care is no longer administered and billed on a per-day basis for as many days as the doctor and patient agree are required; rather, payment is predetermined according to the original diagnosis, regardless of length of stay. Medicare presets payment for a standard number of days it will allow for treatment (barring complications) of each condition—and allows no more.

Because hospitals receive a fixed amount for reimbursement, it behooves hospital personnel to remedy your parent's acute medical problem and discharge him or her as quickly as possible. This has spawned a new care industry called rehabilitation post-hospitalization. For further care, your parent goes to a rehabilitation setting, either as an inpatient at a facility, or, if possible, as an outpatient in a relative's or in his or her own home, where assistance from home-health agencies is provided. The rehabilitation center, not the hospital, serves as your parent's "home" until he or she is ready to go home.

As part of this new approach, hospital social workers, who used to help families work through the process of caring for an elderly relative, have a new function. Because of DRGs, discharge planning is their primary responsibility—sometimes their only responsibility. They offer guidance and support to the family while the doctor gets your mom or dad discharged as soon as possible. In the best scenario, the social work staff helps the family decide on a rehabilitation setting and helps share the burden of dealing with an ill relative.

But the reality is that you're often told, "Your mom broke her hip. The normal length of stay in the hospital is eight days. This is day two; we anticipate discharging her next Thursday. She won't be able to go home by herself. Unless you plan on providing care in your home, you must locate a nursing-home bed for her. Here is a list

7

of nursing homes in the area for you to contact. We hope you'll find one with an opening."

Suddenly, with no advance warning, you must make decisions, with little time, less information, and a minimum amount of guidance to help you.

It is our job to help you understand this new situation so you can best help your parent. We'll try and take everything one logical step at a time, from what you should bring with you when leaving town when responding to the immediate crisis, to dealing with the sibling whose response to your news that mom will now need to be provided with in-home, supervised care is, "You were always her favorite. You handle it."

(NOTE: We often talk about "mom," because, for folks who are eighty-five, that really is the population at risk here. At this age women outnumber men four to one. Of course, everything contained in these pages can be applied equally to dad or anyone else for whom you are providing care.)

Because it is the hardest to handle, we'll deal with the acute-health situation first, then the non-acute or degenerative situation.

The acute crisis

Inevitably, the acute crisis, when emergency care is given to your parent, requires your presence. Whose presence exactly? It requires somebody who's most concerned about seeing to the best interests of the parent. Does that mean everyone, all the parent's children? Probably not. As a simple rule, if the situation is critical, at least one of the children needs to be there. If the situation is serious, though perhaps not life threatening, but you still *feel* you should be there, then go, if for no other reason than your own peace of mind.

(Remember, too, airlines may charge you the lowest fare they offer on a particular route in the case of catastrophic medical events, as long as you are able to provide proof, such as a letter from your parent's doctor. Check with the airline for details and requirements.)

But what if family or work demands are such that you just can't go? What too, if your siblings can't or won't go either, or if you have no siblings? How can you best manage the crisis from afar? Poorly at best, is the honest answer. The crisis requires your presence. It's as simple as that. This is not a situation that can be fully appreciated, assessed, evaluated, and acted on at a distance. It is a time when major decisions have to be made. Remember, however, once you've made the decisions, once you've facilitated hospital care, post-hospital arrangements, and so on, then you can manage them from a distance, with telephone calls to the home-health agency or rehabilitation center. You don't have to be present during that whole process, because it is a process that can (and often does) run from weeks to months (and sometimes longer).

You can only do so much advance preparation for your absence, especially if you get an unexpected call at 10 p.m., and are on a plane at 7 a.m. the following morning. There will be little opportunity to speak with your office, clients, and family. But there are some things you can and should do before leaving.

If you're employed, contact your employer. Explain

what has happened and that you need to leave to manage the situation. Further, though you're not quite sure how long you'll be gone, you will call within twenty-four hours after you have assessed the situation. Though each situation is unique, you should anticipate being away for at least three days, and four or five on average. Pack your bags and take comfortable, easy-to-care-for clothes and especially walking shoes—you'll need them.

In addition to contacting your office, you need to:

• Make two lists. The first should include things that need to be done while you're away. You can have others (spouse, siblings, children, perhaps an assistant or secretary) do the work; you just provide the information. (By the way, you'll be surprised at how helpful people can and will be during a crisis. Just try not to load too much responsibility on anyone's shoulders.) The second list includes information to help you manage your parent's situation, such as:

Name and phone number of his or her primary-care physician

Name, address, and phone number of hospital

Names of consulting and attending specialists

Work and home phone numbers for siblings and others you'll need to call from the hospital

• Decide where you will stay while caring for your parent. In a hotel? You'll need to make reservations. In your parent's home? Make sure you have a key, or can get one.

• Make a "tickler" sheet of things that need to be done

(even though you won't know much of what will be required until you reach the hospital) such as any information you need to give to your parent's landlord, building or facility manager: how to handle mom's mail, daily newspaper delivery, appointments and obligations, her insurance agent, and so on.

• Bring along any legal or financial papers that may be needed, such as advanced life directives, durable power of attorney for health care decisions, and so on. (See Chapter 6 for details.)

• Contact your parent's primary-care office, not to speak with the doctor (you want to, but it's unrealistic to think you will) but to find out when he or she will next be at your mother's bedside. You can plan to meet there. At the very least, make sure the doctor knows you are coming and will set aside some time for you when he or she arrives at the hospital.

• Don't try to talk to the doctor over the phone at this point. He or she is dealing with patients and fielding other phone calls. If it's important enough for you to get on a plane and fly to Chicago, it's important enough for you to be at the hospital at 4:30 in the afternoon if that's when the doctor will be in your mother's room to talk the situation over.

• Understand when doctors are in hospitals. Internists make rounds early in the morning (between 7:30 and 9 a.m.) and late in the afternoon or early evening (between 4:30 and 6:30 p.m.). If you want to talk to the doctor, don't show up at 11 a.m. and expect to find him or her there waiting for you. Though the hospital staff may not be thrilled to see you on the floor at 7:30 a.m. when they are trying to get patients fed and treatments started, if that's when the doctor said he or she is available, you need to be there.

• Make a list of the questions you want to ask the doctor. Though more questions will naturally come up, start with the most obvious:

What is the diagnosis?

What is the recommended treatment?

What is the anticipated discharge date?

Will post-hospitalization care be needed? What kind?

Once you arrive at the hospital, the medical problems, discharge-planning procedure, and resources you'll need to plan your parent's care will become clearer. Find out the name of the social worker or discharge planner at the hospital who is assigned to your parent. Talk to him or her while you are waiting for the doctor to arrive. Social workers' schedules are much more flexible than the doctor's, since they work full time at the hospital and their primary role is to help you help the patient.

Whether talking to the doctor or social worker, be sure to write down what is said to you and expected of you. Be especially careful to record the doctor's answers. This way you can share that information with your siblings, spouse, and others over the phone. Unless the situation is cut-and-dry—mom broke her hip and it needs to be replaced—you absolutely do not want to be reconstructing information from memory, because in a crisis situation you hear about half of what is said, and then retain only about half of that, leaving you with 25 percent of the data.

The non-acute situation

The crisis of an acute medical event and hospitalization compels you to action. It is not, however, the only way in which "the call" comes.

Let's say mom has been going to Dr. Smith for years, but she is becoming increasingly frail. Again, because you live in the next town, you see mom two to three times per week as part of your normal routine—on your way home from work or between dropping the kids off at activities. You notice that mom, who is living independently, is not doing as well as she had been. It is more difficult for her to get to the store, to cook her own meals, or otherwise maintain her lifestyle. You realize she's forgetting to take her medicine and to turn off appliances. You begin thinking about things you hoped you wouldn't have to. You're faced with a role reversal: mom needs you to care for her.

First, have your mother evaluated by a qualified professional, such as a geriatrician or a geriatric psychiatrist, to see if any problems are beyond physical health. You can find these doctors in private practice, through your local hospital's outpatient services, or at a university medical center. (See Part Three: Resources and References for details.)

Once your mother is evaluated, you'll have a better

idea of the care needed and whether you can continue to meet your parent's needs by yourself. If mom can't manage by herself, you'll no doubt say, "Wait a minute. How am I supposed to juggle a career, my own family, and now the care of my parent?" Fifteen years ago, the answer was simply that mom came to live with you, as there were few real alternatives available. Even an assisted-care or nursing facility was hardly an option; there weren't that many nursing beds available.

Now there are a variety of services available: congregate living, assisted living, continuing to live at home with home-health aides or companions, intermediate care-level nursing settings, skilled nursing-care settings, lifecare settings, lifecare settings with attached nursing homes, and so on. Chapter 3 defines some of these options; also refer to Part Three: Resources and References for names of organizations and professionals who can help you.

Once you take the first step and have mom fully evaluated, appropriate options will become clearer.

Chapter 2

Prioritizing & Managing the Acute Crisis and Recognizing the Non-Acute Situation

*O*ne morning, our office received a call from the Employee Assistance Program coordinator of a multinational corporation in Connecticut. One of the company's employees just learned that her father had been hospitalized following a car accident. The employee, a single woman and only child, was upset. She did not know what to do and needed someone to talk to. Our conversation revealed that her father was seventy-eight, retired, and living in Arizona. He had broken his leg in the accident, was confused, and in need of surgery. The hospital in Arizona had called his daughter for her consent to perform surgery. The woman felt overwhelmed. She was 2,500 miles away. Should she go to Arizona? Why did her father need surgery? Was she overreacting? We suggested she inform her boss of the situation and that she needed to be absent from work for a few days. Next, we advised her to telephone her father's physician to gather any information she could. Then, to make airline reservations, pack *a bag for a four-day stay, and to call us back after she had arrived, seen her father and spoken face-to-face with the doctors and nurses in charge of care for her father.*

Relax, then do your best

After you arrive at your parent's bedside (or even as you are making your way there), you'll undoubtedly ask yourself, "What am I supposed to do? Am I doing enough? What does mom expect from me? What do my siblings, relatives, other parent, the medical staff caring for mom expect me to do? How can I actually make a difference in her care? What happens now?"

First, try to relax. This anxiety is very natural. You're traveling in unfamiliar territory, and you're scared. It really is going to be all right. As emotionally and physically demanding as caring for an infirm parent is, it is important to keep the issues at hand in perspective.

• Don't doubt your commitment. After all, between work, family, home, and your own self, who isn't "really busy"? It's always easier to find excuses and just let someone else handle everything. But in spite of what some people may later suggest, or that you may at times feel, the very fact that you are reading this book and assuming responsibility indicates you love your parent and are committed to their care.

• Just do your best. All anyone has any right to expect is that you'll try and do your best on your parent's behalf.

And what is doing your best? Remember the Me Rule. It means that you are always going to do for your parent what you believe they would do for themselves if they could. That's all.

• Gather and disseminate. Think of your parent's care as a tactical maneuver. You're the scout. It is your job to gather as much information and report back to headquarters so that appropriate action can be taken. You are not expected to decide what action is appropriate or carry out that decision alone. Rather, you will share the information you gather and then, as a group, you will reach a consensus, relay that decision to the doctor or other professional, and hope for the best.

Remember, it is not your job to know more about the causes or treatment of your parent's condition than the doctor. You aren't expected to stand at the surgeon's side during the procedure and offer guidance. Nor are you expected, faced with an otherwise routine medical situation, to move your parent into a world-renowned medical facility and employ round-the-clock nurses or otherwise spend money extravagantly on your parent's care so that everyone can plainly see what a caring, loving child you are. Bottom line: Remember the Golden Rule or Me Rule: Do unto others as you would have others do unto you.

Stabilize, then gather information

Your first job is to stabilize the situation before tackling long-term care for your parent. This, of course, is the responsibility of the doctors and medical staff in the hospital.

With straightforward situations (such as a hip fracture replacement case), the doctors can usually give you a sense of what the outcome is going to be. They may tell you one, mom has broken her hip because of a fall (as opposed to any underlying disease or other condition requiring further treatment), and two, she'll have surgery tomorrow. Barring complications, she'll be in the hospital for six more days, then will be discharged to an appropriate setting (nursing home, your home) for rehabilitation.

Now, assuming that you are satisfied that mom is in good hands (both the doctor and facility are acceptable to you), your role at this point is very clear and your marching orders are greatly simplified. In addition to providing bedside comfort and support, you must find a place for mom to go once she's discharged. Later, we'll discuss how you decide where mom should go (into a local facility, into a facility near you or another sibling, home with you for in-home rehabilitation, etc.). For now, however, let's assume that mom's condition is more severe, or the diagnosis is more complicated than the hip fracture described above. How do your actions differ?

First, remember that although you may be the one on scene, it is not your job to make unilateral decisions about your parent's care, even if the medical staff or your siblings attempt to force this responsibility on you. Your job, as the point person, is still to gather as much information as possible to enable everyone to make reasonable and prudent decisions. We say decisions, because inevitably it is not a single issue that must be resolved, such as whether to operate (which, of course, can be a difficult decision on its own). The entire process of providing care is like the ever-branching tree: Each decision opens onto additional areas that need to be addressed, meaning more decisions.

Understand that the potential downside of your making unilateral decisions increases every time you do it. Each time you announce to your siblings "This is what I've done" rather than "Here's what we need to discuss," you are providing an opportunity for everyone else to question your decisions. Sometimes it will seem far more efficient for you to make decisions yourself, and others will want you to make them, thus relieving them of responsibility (while able and ready to point the finger later). We strongly recommend you resist this pressure and always strive for consensus. The only exception to this rule is when you are faced with an acute life-or-death situation. Here you clearly don't have time to gather and consult. You have to act.

Two more reasons for involving others in decisions: Everyone, especially those who aren't onsite, can feel they are a part of the caring process, and, perhaps more important, can share the outcome if the decision results in unforeseen complications. Sharing the decision-making process minimizes whatever guilt you and everyone else will undoubtedly feel. Though it might not make a tragedy easier to accept, at least you won't have to hear, "You took it upon yourself to go ahead and have the doctors do X and look what happened. We never would have agreed to that action."

It may make perfect sense to you, without consulting anyone else, to agree to subject mom to surgery if the doctor tells you that without it she'll be dead in six to twelve months. If however, she dies during the procedure, everyone (including you) is going to think the decision to operate was made hastily. If however, everyone, rather than you alone, backed that decision, it will make life much easier for everyone afterward, regardless of the consequences.

Know what your parent wants

This decision-making process is made easier if you have some sense of what your parent would want done, regardless of whether these wishes are formally expressed in a "living will." (Such documents are discussed in detail in Chapter 6.) If possible, ask your parent how they feel about heroic measures, such as life-support machines, cardiac resuscitation, etc., that can be taken to help them. Be sure to address this issue as soon as your parent is able to.

Learn from this experience. If you have never asked other relatives about this, do so at the earliest possible opportunity. This really isn't as difficult as it may seem. Keep in mind that you aren't advocating a particular course of action; you are merely attempting to learn the individual's wishes so you can, if required, ensure those wishes are respected. Also, let others know how you feel about your own care under such circumstances. Doing so will prevent someone else from being caught in the same quandary you may now find yourself.

How doctors have changed

Assuming that your parent either hasn't prepared a living will or otherwise made her wishes known, or that you can't get the answers you need from her, you and your "action team" of family members will need to make some hard decisions. Start gathering information with your parent's physician. (And don't forget the nurses—our personal and professional experience shows that the nursing staff is one of the best sources of information regarding your parent's present and potential long-term care. Rely on them, confide in them, and you will not be disappointed.)

If you've followed our suggestion in Chapter 1, you have a bedside appointment with the doctor to review mom's condition. Families often assume that because they are now dealing with a stranger and not with good ol' Doc Smith, who was always concerned and available, that the doctor treating mom will be unwilling to give them the time required to answer their questions and help them cope with this crisis.

If this is your fear, you'll probably be in for a pleasant surprise. Our experience has shown that, frantic schedule demands not withstanding, doctors and other health care professionals are as committed to treating people now as they were back when you were dealing with Doc Smith. Doctors making rounds are readily available to sit with families for as long as it takes to help them fully understand the situation and the implications of decisions that need to be made.

The notion that a doctor is only interested in treating

illness, regardless of the impact the treatment has on the quality of the patient's life, is no longer true. Most medical schools have moved toward teaching ethics and other quality-of-life issues. To make logical decisions, lean on the primary-care physician and the other specialists. Because comprehensive geriatric assessment services and professionals—geriatric internists, geriatric psychiatrists, social workers, nurse clinicians, physical therapists, dieticians—have developed throughout this country, getting quality information and direction is much easier. These professionals appreciate the specific issues that impact the elderly and can often help families in concert with their private physicians to make suitable decisions.

That said, you also have to recognize that a doctor is an individual. You need to evaluate and factor in the doctor's own personality and biases when it comes to evaluating treatment for your parent. You can't blindly accept, without question, everything the doctor tells you is the best or the worst for mom. You and your family are the patient's advocates, representing the patient's wishes, desires, and concerns, especially if the patient is incapable of expressing them. Further, if you are prepared with your list of questions, the doctor will appreciate both your desire to be fully informed as well as your preparedness.

Getting your questions answered

Though the specific questions you will need to ask vary depending on your parent's condition, age, and medical history, these basic issues can be addressed:

- What's wrong?
- What caused the current situation or condition?
- What is the recommended treatment?
- Are there alternatives to consider?
- Will any post-hospital care be required?
- If yes, what type and for how long?
- Is there a facility you can recommend?
- If the recommended treatment is followed, what is the long-term outlook for my parent?

Understand that the answer to any of these questions may suggest several follow-up questions. Ask them. Also, if there are unresolved questions regarding the diagnosis or treatment (for example, the doctor really isn't sure what caused mom's current problem, or perhaps she's a candidate for a particularly specialized or difficult surgical procedure), this is the time to satisfy, in your own mind, that mom receives the proper attention.

How do you know if the doctor or facility are the best available? In many localities and in particularly acute situations there is often no real choice but to have mom treated by this doctor in this facility. Other times, you may want to move mom to another hospital or bring in specialists to consult on her care. How do you decide that the time has come to call in specialists or for mom to receive treatment elsewhere?

Again, it's vital that you recognize your role. You are mom's surrogate. Your concern should not be with the doctor's feelings or with expediency. Ask yourself, does what I'm hearing the doctor say make sense? Does the recommended treatment seem prudent? A bizarre diagnosis or recommendation for an intricate surgical procedure is legitimate cause for concern. Use the Me Rule. Ask yourself, "If I were the patient, would I accept what I am being told? Would this make sense to me?" Consider all the facts. If you were eighty-five and in poor health would you want to undergo extensive testing to find the root cause of your condition? Would you be willing to undergo risky or radical therapy or surgery without a second opinion? Whatever the answer, it's fair to assume mom would feel the same way.

Share these feelings with the doctor and get these questions resolved. Consider getting a second opinion. The doctor is not going to have a problem with your desire to consult with other professionals. It's done every day. You aren't questioning the doctor's abilities, but it is you and your family who will have to live with the results of mom's treatment.

Another legitimate concern is time, both from your perspective as well as your parent's. In addition to getting mom started on the road to recovery, you have a life that can't be left on hold indefinitely either. If the boss expects you back for the big client meeting in four days, then you need answers and you need them now. Don't be shy; explain this to the doctor. You'll want to get the answers you need and have a course of action agreed upon before you depart. Even so, you will likely be engaged in a fair amount of second guessing, especially if the decisions made by everyone results in some unfortunate consequences. You can't worry too much about that; you want to be able to say, "I got opinions from the top people available (or at the best facility available) and everyone concurred on mom's treatment." That's the most you can do, and that's fine.

Aside from specialists and other practitioners providing second opinions, what other options can you consider for your parent's care? With unusual medical problems, we often defer to the university hospital setting and its superior resources, especially for those conditions we feel are beyond the expertise of local hospitals and physicians. For example, suppose neurosurgical intervention is required to remove a questionable tumor (which is the cause of mom's falling and hip fracture). Should mom remain at the local facility and undergo the surgery, or should you consider moving her to a higher-profile institution? Even though the local neurosurgeon is technically qualified to perform the surgery, you may find that the act of simply transferring mom to a facility where an abundance of such procedures are performed may help you to sleep better at night, regardless of the outcome.

We keep talking about the consequences of surgery (and virtually any procedure or treatment) because all surgery carries some degree of risk. That risk (the chief risk being the possibility that mom doesn't survive the procedure) is increased with advanced age and the more precarious health of the patient. Surgery and its risks must be considered very carefully. You can usually count on the doctor for guidance. If the procedure is especially risky (or if your parent's age is sufficiently advanced), the doctor will probably raise the risk-benefit issue before you think about it. Further, the doctor will also want to know

25

how the family feels about drastic life-saving procedures, should these be necessary. If mom has left either a living will or at least made her wishes known to you and or the rest of the family, the decision is much easier.

To repeat, the three most important things to remember are:

- You are acting, at all times, as your parent's advocate and surrogate.

- Unless your parent's condition demands immediate action, avoid making any decisions until all pertinent information is gathered.

- No decisions should be made unilaterally. Whenever possible, all decisions should be made after reaching a consensus with family members.

Not everyone can be involved

Often, mom's other children who are not onsite will want to speak with her attending physician themselves. Though this may seem like the best way to put everyone at ease while taking some of the weight off your shoulders, it probably isn't practical. First, the reason you are there is to get all the information. Second, getting you together with the doctor in the first place was hard enough. Can you imagine coordinating that effort three or four more times?

Let's look at a specific example. At eighty-four, Ralph G. developed congestive heart failure, went into respiratory distress, and was rushed from the senior-housing facility where he lived to the local hospital. Doctors put him on a respirator and graded his condition as critical.

The first family member to arrive, a grandchild and a physician, told the doctors she didn't want any heroic measures undertaken on his behalf. Six hours later, when the second grandchild (also a physician) arrived and evaluated the situation, he promptly reversed the earlier instruction, saying that it was premature to have made such a decision, and wanted the medical staff to aggressively treat his grandfather's condition. A short time later, a third grandchild (yet another physician) who lived one thousand miles away, called, spoke with the other two grandchildren, learned about the care conflict, and demanded to speak with the attending physician to evaluate the situation and make his own recommendation. At this point, the poor doctor, who had been even more forthcoming with information because he's dealing with a group of doctors, simply throws up his hands and says, "Look, I appreciate that everyone's concerned about Grandpa. But, please, be fair. Who's in charge? Who am I supposed to actually listen to here?"

A family has the responsibility to appoint one representative to gather information and share it with the other siblings, and not to make decisions before everyone has been consulted, unless an immediate response is required.

Interestingly, Ralph's case points up not only the various medical disciplines of the grandchildren (the first is a pediatrician, the second a geriatric psychiatrist, the third a pathologist) but also their different personalities and their relationship with their grandfather, and how all this figures in the decision-making process. It was much more difficult for the first relative, who was there in the early, acute stages to deal with the entire situation. It was emotionally overwhelming for her. Often, because a relative may be enduring tremendous pain and suffering, it's very natural to say, "I can't bear to see my parent suffer like this. Don't do anything. Please, for their sake, for mine—let it just be over." The implication of making such an emotionally charged decision, however, can be enormous. In Ralph's case, he lived nine more years after this crisis.

Know the statistics

One tool that can help you make decisions is the life-expectancy tables used by the insurance industry to price its policies. Let's examine one potential scenario: If a white, middle-class woman in America has lived to the age of sixty-five, she can reasonably expect to live nineteen more years. Essentially, nearly a quarter of her life is before her. If she's lived to seventy-five, she has fourteen more years of life expectancy. If she's eighty-five, she can expect to live nine more years. See life expectancy table on page 149.

Many people will be surprised by these numbers. They are apt to make life-and-death decisions based on antiquated or naive perceptions of aging and longevity. Thinking to yourself, "Well, Dad died at seventy-two, Mom's now seventy-six, I guess she can't live much longer," is simply not accurate. In fact, unless she suffers a health crisis, she may have as many as fourteen more years of life to live. Understanding this, you quickly realize it may be inappropriate to withhold potentially lifesaving care based on your own personal discomfort along with mistaken notions about your parent's life expectancy.

One-on-one care

As you sit by mom's bedside, you may find that mom isn't receiving the individualized care and attention that you'd like. Welcome to modern medicine. Be assured that her medical and comfort needs will be met, but nurses tending to patients in an overcrowded, understaffed facility just aren't able to give one-on-one care. That's why you may want to consider hiring private duty nurses. This is a very expensive service, roughly $15 per hour, $120 per shift or $350-$400 per day, above and beyond daily hospital charges if you have twenty-four-hour coverage. Though expensive, private nursing care may be money well spent in certain cases. If you're only going to be in town for a few days and need to get a lot accomplished, a private nurse can fill in for you. If the bad time for mom is evenings, perhaps you only need to have someone there from 3 to 11 p.m. or 4 p.m. to midnight to help out through the acute hospitalization period.

In addition to providing mom with the additional attention and companionship you'd like her to have, it can also provide a certain comfort simply to know that the same person is going to be there every day to provide you with an update on the situation. This is an improvement over learning that the very pleasant, professional floor nurse who was taking care of mom is now off for three days.

Talking to your parent

You've made your evaluations, shared the information with the rest of your family, and have made those wishes known to the doctors. But your parent may still be in the dark about their own condition. How much do you actually tell your parent?

It depends on your parent's ability to comprehend and interpret this information. In the best of circumstances, you'll be able to present the data in full, openly and objectively. However, you may have to approach this discussion in a manner not unlike the parent whose five-year-old has just asked where babies come from. You supply enough information to satisfy the question without supplying more detail than can be understood or assimilated at this point. But, of course, this isn't a child but a mature adult we're talking about. Again, use the Me Rule. If you were the patient you'd want to know the truth. So does your parent. Say something like, "Mom, when you fell you broke your hip. It has to be replaced. The doctors want to operate Thursday. After that you'll be in the hospital for a few more days. Then, since you'll have trouble walking, you're not going to be able to go home immediately. You'll need to go to a nursing home where you'll be able to get the physical therapy that will help get you up and on your feet."

It probably won't be an enjoyable conversation, but it

is the plain truth. While there is no need to sugarcoat this information, it is equally important that you don't project your own fears or negative assumptions to your parent. Aside from possibly frightening your parent unnecessarily, you simply don't know what the outcome will be. Circumstances may dictate that given her other medical problems, your mother may never return to her own home. But if this is indeed the case, it will become apparent during rehabilitation. That is the appropriate time to deal with this situation.

After hospitalization

Perhaps your parent has been living in some type of senior housing. What becomes of her home during the rehabilitation period? There's no easy answer, because each case is unique. If your parent bought into a lifecare setting then she will be going into its nursing home for rehabilitation while retaining ownership of her unit. In most instances, the resident is allowed anywhere from sixty to ninety days in the rehabilitation setting before a decision must be made. So there's no rush to give your parent's apartment or living unit up. If your parent lives in another type of senior housing (perhaps underwritten by the Department of Housing and Urban Development [HUD] or other government agency), you simply continue to pay rent until alternative arrangements are made.

Remember that after an acute-care hospital stay, Medicare will pay for up to one hundred days of post-hospital nursing home care for acute rehabilitation. Medicare will also pay for home health and rehabilitation services in your or your parent's home. But Medicare will suspend coverage if the physical therapist, the attending physician, or other specialists involved in rehabilitation determine that your parent won't be getting any better. Overall, Medicare only pays for about 2 percent of long-term care stays. And your parent has to be hospitalized for seventy-two hours before entering a rehabilitation setting to be eligible for Medicare payments. (More details on the Medicare system appear in Chapter 3.)

The key here is to not make unreasonable assumptions since you don't know what will happen three months down the road. Anticipate positive outcomes, but be aware of negative consequences. Try not to project your notions of eldercare onto your parent. Not all nursing homes are potentially abusive warehouses for the elderly. At their best, nursing homes are essential institutions that provide a level of care and a sense of safety and comfort for patients that may not exist for them anywhere else.

A nursing home isn't your only option, however. Even if her doctor determines that mom needs acute nursing and rehabilitative care for a couple of weeks or even months to stabilize her condition, it is possible to provide that care at home if you or another relative are willing to take on the responsibility. Because mom's been hospitalized for an acute situation, Medicare will pay for a good portion of the "medically necessary equipment and services" after mom's discharge, which may include the rental of a hospital bed, bedside commode, wheelchair, walker, and so on, providing these are authorized by the doctor. Certainly this is easier to accomplish if you and mom live in the same community, a little bit more difficult in distant communities. The paperwork procedures, however, are the same either way.

If the parent is alone, she is often moved to a place closest to the child who has assumed responsibility. It is not unusual, for example, to have patients undergo hospitalization in Florida and be admitted to a long-term care facility in New York because a son or daughter lives there. Again, make sure the family is consulted and that everyone is as comfortable with the decision as possible.

The primary issue here is managing the *responsibility,* not only for providing the hands-on care required but for managing the financial impact as well. If one child (or other relative) takes on the demands of providing the physical care, the financial responsibility for that care falls to those siblings who can't take mom into their homes.

Note that we say "can't" rather than "won't." Your brother argues that he's is too far away and too busy. Your sister also lives far away and is always on the road and isn't available to provide care. In truth, if you weren't there they would be doing the work, but they won't have to because you have assumed the responsibility. A long-distance family conference with the guidance of a geriatric specialist can be a great device for working out a mutually agreeable arrangement. This may mean presenting a scenario to your siblings that you find equitable, such as, "Mom will move into my home. I'll need $220 a week for home-health aides; that's $110 a week each." And if they balk and say, "Gee that's an awful lot of money every week," your response may have to be, "Fine. Mom will be on the first plane to you. You provide the care in your home. I'll be sure to send along my first check."

It may seem harsh, but if you present the situation in these terms, your family will be much more understanding about what needs to be done.

Families who really work together to manage the situation will come up with a complete plan for sharing responsibility. Those not providing daily care will either fly in to spell the caregiver, or provide funding so that the caregiver can arrange a much-needed break for themselves. Such are the fruits of up-front negotiations.

To summarize the points made in this chapter:

- Stabilize the patient.
- Deal with the situation.
- Gather information.
- Share the information with your siblings, relatives, and parent.
- Evaluate the situation and reach a consensus.
- Act on your decision.
- Prepare post-hospitalization arrangements.

Chapter 3

What Kind of Care?

Susan wasn't sure how much longer she could take it. For the last eight months she had been juggling her job, her family, and the care of both her mother and her husband's aunt. At first it didn't seem so bad. Her mother lived only two miles away and wasn't really in need of much help—little errands to pick up groceries, some driving to get to the doctors, some cooking assistance, mostly companionship. Aunt Jean was another story. She lived in an old farmhouse twenty minutes away and needed help with just about everything. Susan wasn't sure if Aunt Jean should be living alone, but she was so difficult no one knew what to do with her.

To get everything done, Susan was up by 5:30 a.m. By 7:45 she had the kids ready for school, her husband off to work, and her own day was just beginning. On the way to work, Susan drove out to Aunt Jean's house to help her dress and set food for the day out on the counter. If it were left in the refrigerator, Aunt Jean simply forgot to eat. Susan couldn't stay with her aunt long and felt guilty, having to cut her short when she *was in the middle of some story about a favorite TV show or the days when Uncle Don was still alive. But she couldn't afford to be late getting to the office. That had happened too many times.*

The phone rang at 11 p.m. and James reluctantly answered it. The voice on the other end explained that his father had once again decided to take an evening walk in the pleasant California night air, only to get lost and not return. Police found him walking in a downtown area. The director of his father's continuing-care residence told James that it had become a problem for them to be out looking for his wandering, disoriented father. He was no longer suited for the independent lifestyle of the complex and James would have to solve his father's living situation quickly. As he hung up the phone, James felt frustrated and fatigued. This had been going on for months, but he didn't know what to do. His job in New York was demanding and his father in California seemed a world away.

How do you know when care is needed?

Signs that additional assistance is needed come from either the person receiving care or from the caregiver. Often these signs go undetected. Or, a caregiver may recognize the time has come to seek backup help, but barriers exist to obtain the help easily. The following lists some of the signals indicating the time has come to look for new, changed, or expanded support systems. The list is not definitive; every household and family will have its own situation. Time to provide care, distance from the relative requiring care, previous relationships with the elderly person, and financial resources will all influence the choices made.

Avoid thinking, however, that one person and one person alone must become responsible for the care; this can become very defeating, as needs, guilt, and fatigue will all increase. You don't need to face this situation alone. If you don't have siblings or other relatives, contact a professional organization that deals with eldercare issues. Obtaining help to care for a parent is not a sign of weakness or neglect on your part. Adult children must be clear as to what they can and should be doing for a parent, and how they can help each other provide that care. Many times it is best to remain the daughter or a son and let a trained professional assume the responsibility of direct-care provider.

Signs that indicate the need for additional care

The caregiver has:

- Missed work repeatedly to provide care
- Lost sleep on a regular basis
- Stopped his or her own social activities because of the demands of caregiving
- Discovered his or her time with members of the immediate family has been replaced by caregiving

- Begun to resent caregiving
- Begun to feel overwhelmed by the amount of care he or she must provide
- Become ill or unable to keep up with caregiving
- Traveled too far to provide care

The elderly person has:

- Become very forgetful and suffers memory loss
- Become unsafe alone or in his or her living arrangement
- Stopped eating when alone
- Fallen or is at a high risk of falling
- Forgotten to take important medications
- Stopped socializing and has become isolated
- Become incontinent
- Wandered out of the house and become confused or disoriented
- Become combative or had other significant personality changes
- Become unsafe when driving a car

Consider additional help or a change in your parent's current living situation if any of the above applies. Take stock not only of your parent's welfare but your own physical and emotional state as well. You'll do no one any good if you deny your own needs.

What kind of care does your parent need?

The process of recognizing a change and seeking help may come around many times, because the degree of care required by an elderly person changes over time. Be prepared to modify the initial solution you settle on.

At the simplest level, your parent may require nothing more than someone to help with basic daily household duties: housekeeping, meal preparation, laundry, driving, reminders to take medications, and socializing. A homemaker or a companion, terms used by the home-health care industry, can perform these tasks for your parent. These workers are not certified and there are no state-mandated training programs for them. Many have taken workshops or classes on caring for the elderly offered by a home-health agency or other health care employer as part of an agency's employment requirements.

In most states, homemakers and companions are not intended to provide any personal care, such as bathing, dressing, feeding, and toilet needs. If personal care is required, a home-health aide or nurse is usually hired. Home-health aides, trained to deliver personal care to an older person, are certified by attending a recognized program and successfully passing various examinations.

Many states have clear laws stating who is qualified and can legally deliver personal care. If a person is not able to care for himself or herself, the assumption is that there should be legal protection for the well-being of that person. Thus, personal care should be planned under the direction of a registered nurse, even when it is carried out by an aide. This is called skilled-nursing care. It is illegal in some states for aides to practice independently, which means a nursing or home-health agency must plan and set up care for your parent.

This becomes a catch-22 for many families. The laws that are in place to protect them can also limit choices. Technically, if someone needs help dressing, skilled nursing would be required, but a companion or homemaker can competently assist in dressing in many cases. Make sure the responsibilities you ask a companion to assume are not outside the boundaries of what they can legally perform.

Family members will need to decide, keeping in mind that if a companion or homemaker is brought in without skilled-nursing supervision, they will need to recognize when more skilled care becomes necessary. In this chapter, we'll define some services and agencies to help you evaluate the proper level of care for your parent. In Chapter 4, you'll learn how to hire a helper for your parent. First, you need to determine what your parent needs. Home care (as opposed to nursing-home care) is appropriate when:

- Care can be delivered in the home to ensure safety and rehabilitation.

- The level of care needed is less expensive in the home than in a nursing home.

- The person requiring care is adamantly opposed to entering a nursing home.

- The person requiring care is competent to make decisions about where care should be provided.

- You are prepared to accept some of the anxiety and ambiguity that goes along with home care versus nursing-home care.
- Health care professionals believe that home care can serve the needs of the person requiring care.

If an individual is able to remain at home, consider three basic types of care:

- Full-time or part-time assistance in the home during some part of the day or night
- Adult day care or a form of respite care, in which your parent goes out of the house to participate in a program for the day or part of the day
- Live-in help or help that comes into the home round-the-clock

Determining required assistance

One easy method for deciding is to create a table describing the tasks that need to be managed. Give careful and honest thought to what your parent can do alone or unsupervised; what you realistically can do; what needs to be done by someone else; the time of day or night these tasks need to be done; and how often care is needed during the week. You will quickly see what type and when additional coverage is needed. The table can be expanded if hours of the day or night differ from day to day. An example follows:

	Cook meals	Drive car	Supervise dressing	Remind medications	Socializing
MON	needed	not needed	needed	needed	day care
TUES	needed	not needed	needed	needed	needed
WED	needed	needed	needed	needed	day care
THURS	needed	not needed	needed	needed	needed
FRI	needed	not needed	needed	needed	day care
SAT	me	me	me	me	not needed
SUN	me	me	me	me	not needed

This table was developed for a woman whose father lived with her. He was unable to be alone, and she worked during the day and needed assistance for her father during those hours. At first, she thought she needed someone who could drive. But after looking at the weekly demands for transportation, she realized she could solve the driving separately when necessary, and on three weekdays, the adult day care program offered transportation.

Descriptions of specific help

To further help you decide on the appropriate care needed for your parent, we've listed and defined some of the options. They include:

- Hospital-based private duty nurses
- Companions and homemakers
- Home-health aides
- Visiting nurses
- Live-in help (twenty-four hour care)
- Meals on Wheels
- Help paying for prescriptions
- Adult day care
- Partial hospitalization services
- Congregate housing and assisted living
- Retirement centers
- Lifecare centers
- Intermediate-care facilities
- Skilled-nursing care facilities

Hospital-based private duty nurses: These workers are licensed nurses working through an agency that provides in-hospital care in eight-hour shifts. They are not paid for by Medicare, nor paid for by the hospital stay. In some cases, these nurses are paid for by supplemental insurance (discussed in Chapter 5). They provide continuous bedside care for patients. While some feel this is an excessive expense when you're paying as much as you already are for a basic hospital stay, it often provides peace of mind. Cost for a private-duty nurse runs anywhere from $15 to $20 per hour.

Companions and homemakers: These are the least

expensive alternative if mom doesn't need to go to a nursing home after her hospitalization but does require some care at home. These workers are not nurses nor are they licensed. Essentially they provide companionship and can assist with transportation, shopping, cooking, and light housekeeping from four to twelve hours per day. Most are available through private agencies listed under Home-health Agencies in the Yellow Pages. Costs for companions run $5 to $10 per hour, and are often contracted for four hours per day, five days a week ($100-$200). Sometimes, live-in companions are hired to provide twenty-four-hour supervision, for a cost of $300 to $500 a week.

Home-health aides: Usually, these workers are employees of home-health agencies. In most cases, certified and licensed home-health assistants will provide structure and supervision beyond a companion, often assisting with bathing, toilet needs, dressing, and chores around the house. They will also make sure your parent takes her medication on time, although they are not licensed to actually give patients medication. Often the home-health agency's nurses will come in the home and put medications in envelopes with times and dates for the home-health aide to give to the patient. Costs range from $12 to $18 per hour, often for a minimum of two to four hours a day.

Visiting nurses: A licensed nurse, who often supplements a home-health aide, can come in once or twice a week and has supervisory responsibilities, including monitoring care given by home-health aides, checking blood pressure and general physical and mental health, hygiene, and diet, and dispensing medication. A licensed nurse working for a home-health agency can earn as much as $60 per hour when skilled-nursing care is required.

Live-in help: Live-in help is an alternative for those who don't require round-the-clock care but who don't want to place their parent in a nursing home. These workers can be companions, home-health aides, or even licensed nurses. Remember, all these are available only five days a week and you will need to make other plans for the remaining two days.

An elderly person who requires companionship and supervision but not much hands-on care should do well with a companion. For such care as bathing and dressing, you will probably need a home-health aide.

Meals on Wheels provides one or two balanced meals a day, often delivered in the late morning for a hot lunch and later for a microwavable hot dinner. On Fridays these services may deliver multiple meals for the weekend. (If mom has a microwave, it makes life much easier. If she can use it, so much the better. If you plan on buying her one, keep it as simple and gadget-free as possible.) The average cost for such meals runs $4.50 to $8 per meal.

Prescription payment: Based on your parent's economic need, varying from $1 to $2 per prescription or 25 to 30 percent of the actual cost of the prescription. The average elderly individual is taking four prescriptions at once, and so may have a $250 a month pharmacy bill for the cost of those medications. Check with your physician to see whether generic substitutions can be made. For many of the state-funded medical programs, generic drugs are required to be dispensed unless your parent's doctor insists on a brand name.

Adult day care centers: These facilities provide a building, transportation, one hot meal a day, nursing supervision, bathing and toilet assistance, and activities, often on a sliding-fee scale ranging from $5 a day for those living below the poverty line to as much as $60 per day for an eight-hour day. (A discussion of determining ability to pay is in Chapter 5.) Compare the cost of a home-health aide or a nurse to adult day care two, three, four, or even seven days a week for eight hours of consistent, continued, compassionate care. This alternative is probably the best value of all home-health choices.

Partial hospitalization services: Historically limited to patients with a psychiatric diagnosis such as dementia, these services have become popular for patients with depressive disorders and who need post-hospitalization follow-up or a structured therapeutic community that will treat their depression and allow them to return to their previous level of functioning. These services are often reimbursed by Medicare. They are not alternatives to adult day care, however, but are alternatives to extended or initial hospitalization. The average length of stay is four weeks. Often this initial period can be extended another four to eight weeks. Costs run 25 to 50 percent of full-service, in-patient hospital costs, usually $150 to $450 per day. Again, most insurance plans, including Medicare, reimburse for this service because it decreases the length of stay for in-patient care, and thus saves money for the insurance company.

Congregate housing: One of a number of alternatives to living at home—which can mean the caregiver's home, a condominium or apartment, or senior housing—congregate housing is often viewed as independent apartment-type dwellings that you buy or rent. Meals are provided for a fee and a minimum amount of health care supervision is available. A nurse is often on duty during the day to do blood pressure checks, monitor general health, and make sure medications are taken.

Assisted living situations are often in the same complex as congregate housing facilities. Staff companions or home-health aides are placed in the resident's own apartment and provide companionship, assistance, transportation, and, in the case of home-health aides, personal care.

Retirement centers: These differ by the services they provide. In some cases retirement centers simply include your parent's own dwelling with a recreation center and nurses who visit on scheduled days. A clinic with a doctor who comes in one or two days a week to provide health care onsite may be included. Retirement centers often have a cash buy-in, as if you were buying a condo. In some cases that money or 90 percent of the equity is returned if mom needs to leave the congregate / lifecare setting and move to skilled-nursing facilities or into your own home.

Lifecare centers: The concept of lifecare centers, first developed in the late 1970s, provide the housing and caring needs of financially secure elderly people, including dining-room services, activities, and programs, plus a nursing-home unit discreetly placed within the facility. The goal is to prevent nursing-home stays and to make it easier to move a person back to his or her own apartment with additional health-care assistance. Most operate with an upfront purchase of an apartment (costs range from $65,000 to $300,000) and a monthly maintainance fee ($250 to $1,800). This fee pays for meals, activities, and upkeep of grounds and facilities. Sometimes units are available for a monthly rental fee. Nursing-home expenses are included in the up-front purchase price, although this policy varies from state to state and center to center.

Intermediate-care facilities (ICF): These are nursing-home settings with skilled medical personnel, except the patient is independent for washing, bathing, dressing, eating, and toilet needs. Nurses and nurses' aides are on duty twenty-four hours per day. The ICF setting provides a structure and often the best piece of mind when multiple assistance needs can't be pieced together to provide ongoing care at home. Costs range from $75 to $85 per day.

Nursing homes (skilled-nursing facilities): As defined by Medicare and Medicaid, these are for patients requiring twenty-four-hour nursing care, including washing, bathing, dressing, feeding, and medications or treatments. The average skilled-nursing facility in the United States runs about $3,000 per month, or $100 per day. The most expensive facilities run $250 per day or $7,500 per month, or $36,000 to $60,000 a year.

Chapter 4

Locating Care Providers and Evaluating Two: Home Companions and Nursing Homes

D r. M. was a seventy-three-year-old, recently retired family practitioner whose wife had died six years earlier.
He had lived by himself and had continued to practice for awhile,
but eventually he had to stop. Sara was providing twenty-four-
hour care, and she wanted to explore the available services designed to help her father and give her some much-needed relief.
Both Sara and her husband worked full time, and it was unsafe
for dad to remain in their home unsupervised during the day.

Sara ran an advertisement in the local newspaper for a daytime comapnion for her father. She was surprised when she received only three phone calls. Feeling pressured to resolve the
situation, she hired the third person she interviewed. Two days
later, her new employee began caring for her father five days a
week, eight hours a day for $400 each week, cash.

Three weeks into this arrangement, the companion called
in sick and told Sara she was unavailable for the next week.

Frantic, Sara called the EAP (Employee Assistance Program) office at her company and was referred to our office. An emergency evaluation of her father's condition, and a quick referral to the Visiting Nurses Association (VNA) and a local adult daycare center solved Sara's crisis within two days.

The new arrangement was this: Dad went to the daycare center five days a week from 8:15, when the daycare van picked him up, until 3:30 when it dropped him back home. A home-health aide met him and stayed until Sara arrived home from work at 6 p.m. In addition to providing a caring, licensed aide to look after dad, the VNA was available round-the-clock for emergencies.

This solution worked until his symptoms of dementia progressed and he was unable to continue at the adult daycare center. Though Sara and her husband managed for a while, eventually the demands of work, family, and eldercare proved too much. They decided to place dad in a nursing home near one of Sara's sibling's home.

In Chapter 3 we discussed some types of available care and services. In this chapter we'll explore ways you can find help for your parent. We'll also tell you what to look for and what questions to ask, whether you use a service or rely on yourself to find help. To make it simple, we'll concentrate on home companions on one end of the spectrum, then on nursing homes on the other.

Though it seems obvious to say that not every nursing

home is the same, or that every visiting nurse is as compassionate and qualified as another, people seldom know how to go about finding or screening them. But it's worth your efforts to learn. Nothing causes as much anxiety as discovering that a facility or an individual is not giving your parent proper care, or—even worse—that your parent is being mistreated by the care provider you chose and trusted.

Where do you find care?

Do you run an ad in the newspaper? Do you ask everyone you know for suggestions? Do you start with the first listing in the Yellow Pages? Call the local hospital or state office on aging? It can be frustrating to find that right somebody who is going to fit into your or your parent's home. Because people providing care in the home may be working independently, you'll want someone who is not only qualified, experienced, and makes you feel comfortable about leaving your parent in their care, but is reliable, dependable, and has their own transportation to be at work on time each day.

Once you determine the skill level required, you'll need to determine how often they will be needed to provide care. This can vary from hiring a live-in twenty-four hours a day to only needing help occasionally when family or friends are not able to fill in. If the latter is the case, find out if volunteer programs exist in your area that supply assistance with companionship, chores, running errands, shopping and transportation on a short-term, intermittent basis. If routine assistance for longer stretches of time is required, four main choices exist:

- Consult a case manager who brokers and manages home-health services.

- Have a home-health agency evaluate care requirements and then provide someone with the appropriate skill level. The caregiver is an employee of that agency and you pay for services on an hourly basis.

- Have a service that specializes in conducting searches help you find someone who meets your requirements. Once hired, this person becomes your employee. You pay the service a fee.

- Find someone on your own whom you then hire.

There are pros and cons to each of these routes:

- **Using case management:** One of the fastest-growing services for the elderly is case management. In the same way you might hire a service to come in and child-proof your home, case management services, many of which are operated by social workers, come into your home and "elder-proof" it. In addition, working from guidelines established by the National Association of Case Managers, they work with families to broker and manage home-health services. They contract services from the Visiting Nurses Association (VNA), for-profit agencies, and adult day care centers. Check the Yellow Pages for local case management firms, and see Part Three for more resources.

The benefits of case management include minimizing the amount of time you would otherwise spend on deciding on services, as well as on screening and selecting care providers. A case manager has the expertise to help you choose the right adult daycare center and the right doctor for your parent. They also provide transportation to doctor's offices, oversee the running of a your parent's household, including bill-paying. The down side of using case managers is the cost. They may charge an hourly fee ($15-$45) or a flat fee for an initial consultation ($75-$350) plus hourly rates for their time on an on-going basis.

• **Using an agency:** This can be another one-stop shopping option for you. Care can be coordinated if, for example, around-the-clock shifts are required. Also, if anything goes wrong or if the caregiver is ill, the agency is responsible for making sure someone else arrives for work. But remember that the agency's hourly rates can be expensive and may require a minimum number of hours be worked each day. In addition, available shifts may be preset around the agency's schedule, not around your parent's. For instance, the agency may start daytime hours at 8 a.m. What happens if you need someone an hour earlier? Also, if the agency has high employee turnover, you might have a series of people coming through your home. If your parent has memory loss or becomes disoriented easily, this may be confusing. On the other hand, the agency assumes all responsibility for payroll taxes, insurance, and other expenses for their caregivers.

• **Hiring a service to search for a caregiver:** Such a service charges a fee for screening applicants to find the right person to meet your needs, who then becomes your employee. Depending on your requirements, the service may already have a registry of people ready to begin immediately. Be sure a careful assessment of your needs is made, preferably one that includes a home visit. Also, information about your parent's interests and personality should be noted. Be sure to ask for and check all references.

An advantage to having someone else looking on your behalf is that you are saved the time-consuming screening process. But, since this process differs from service to service, don't hesitate to ask exactly what they do and how they do it. Don't be intimidated by the service's personnel. They are there to provide you with a service for which you are paying. Only you know exactly what you need.

Another plus is that since you are directly employing a caregiver, you might have additional flexibility in setting work hours and controlling duties and responsibilities. A very big plus can be the cost. When you pay someone directly, your costs are generally much lower because the overhead costs for personnel, such as that at a home-health agency, are eliminated.

Disadvantages include fees, which can differ greatly among services. Ask for specific details on the fee arrangement before you request assistance. Some states require all placement services to be licensed and have very specific laws regarding what they can and cannot do. For example, licensed placement services in Connecticut are required to guarantee a placement for a ten-week period or provide a replacement or a prorated refund of the fee paid. If you are not dealing with a licensed service, be sure you have some recourse if a problem comes up.

• **Finding your own caregiver:** This can be the least expensive route, but also the most disastrous. Most people start by asking everyone they know about who might be available and recommended. This is a worthwhile method, but it usually doesn't offer enough leads to solve your problem. A newspaper advertisement will undoubtedly bring responses, but it will be up to you to determine who is appropriate for the job.

If you are arranging interviews, you must allow for those who never show up and for those who do and gain information about your home and circumstances. You have eliminated the placement service's fees and the agency's hourly rates, but you have left yourself unprotected. There is no one to run to for a refund or a replacement. You must interview cautiously and check all references. Consider checking police records as well. Remember, you may feel desperate to find someone, but it is your family member who will be left in a stranger's care.

A final consideration for hiring someone on your own is the tax and legal issues. Anyone who acts as an employer is responsible for a portion of FICA (Social Security), for federal unemployment tax, state unemployment tax, and workman's compensation. This sounds worse than it really is. The additional expenses, depending upon the agreed upon salary, can still make this an affordable option.

Ask the right questions

The following is a suggested list of issues to be aware of and questions to ask. Don't let anyone come to your home until you have some basic information. If you use a service, it will be able to provide you with a great deal of data before you meet your potential health care helper.

When using any type of agency, be sure to ask about:

• Method used to determine suitable applicants

• Whether agency personnel meets applicants in person or conducts phone interviews only

• Whether applicants complete a formal application

• Whether references are checked and by whom

• Whether a police record check and a motor vehicle record are obtained. Some agencies charge a fee for this information. Because of privacy laws, some states require that this information be obtained by the person under review and then passed on to you.

• Whether you'll be able to interview applicants who meet your criteria. Some agencies assign applicants to clients.

• Type of contract the agency requires you to sign

• How the agency calculates its fees. Be cautious of a fee that is a multiple of the weekly salary (an amount that may be two or three times the weekly salary of the companion). You may pay a higher salary than necessary using this method.

• Up-front fees. Are you billed only after a companion

has been placed with you, or are there before-placement charges?

• Protection for you if the companion does not remain in your employ. How long are you protected?

• The agency's license. Ask or find out if your state has laws that govern the agency.

• The speed with which they can supply you with applicants

• Turnover rate for companions

• Whether the applicant is an employee of the agency. Also, is he or she insured and bonded?

• What happens if the applicant is hired and is unable to arrive for work one day. Will the agency replace the individual? If so, how quickly?

If you are screening and hiring an employee on your own, start with a telephone conversation. Ask simple questions, such as the person's name, address, and telephone number. Find out about previous work experience, how long he or she was at the last job, and why they left. Obtain the names and telephone numbers of references, especially the applicant's most recent employer. Be wary of anyone with only short-term references or only out-of-state or unavailable references. Ask any questions that will give you a sense of the person and if this is someone you would enjoy having in your home. If you are satisfied, ask the applicant to come to your home for a personal interview and to meet your parent. Ask him or her to bring a police record check, if time allows, or make arrangements to have it sent later. Also, ask for a written list of references with their names and telephone numbers. Before the applicant arrives, verify the spelling and number of their address and phone number.

During the interview, observe the applicant's:

• Ability to arrive on time

• Style of dress. Is it neat, clean, and in keeping with an appearance you are comfortable with?

• Personal hygiene and cleanliness

• Ability to speak clearly and be understood easily

• Ability to handle telephone messages competently (ask how they would handle in-coming calls; also, observe applicant's telephone style during your initial phone conversation)

• Ability to demonstrate an appropriate level of respect and courtesy

• General comfort and willingness to perform the described tasks

• Obtain, in writing, the names, addresses, telephone numbers, and the dates of employment for all references.

Call all the applicant's references and ask:

• When and for how long was the person employed?

• What were the duties and responsibilities?

• How were the duties carried out?

• What problems or difficulties arose?

• What type of temperament or personality does the person have?

• Was the individual punctual and courteous?

• Were there problems with illness, family responsibilities, transportation difficulties, weather conditions, and so on?

• Why did the applicant leave the employment?

• Would the reference hire him or her again?

• Briefly describe the tasks the applicant would be doing for you and ask if they seem appropriate for the applicant's capabilities.

• Is the reference is comfortable recommending this person?

If the interview proceeds well, the references are positive, and you are enthusiastic about the individual, be sure to carefully define the duties and responsibilities for the employee. Many relationships have failed because the employer was expecting duties different from those performed by the employee. The clearer you can be, the less opportunity there is for confusion.

If you have any doubts about the applicant, consider hiring someone on a trial basis. This gives both parties an opportunity to evaluate the situation and make sure all is proceeding well. If you have used an agency, make sure your trial period does not force you to pay an additional placement fee if you decide against keeping the companion.

Here are some questions to guide the orientation process after you've hired your new health care companion.

General Information

• What hours and schedule do you expect the companion to be available? If the companion is needed for assistance

59

early in the morning or for retiring, those times need to be designated. If the companion is a live-in, time of rising and retiring in the evening, should be specified.

• An outline or list of duties to be performed should include how often they are done, such as bringing in the mail daily or changing the bedding once weekly.

• How and when will the companion be paid? Be clear. Will you or the companion be responsible for Social Security and other taxes?

• If shopping is necessary, the handling of money for purchases should be detailed.

• When is time off scheduled? If the companion is a live in, who will cover? (Consider a family member, friend, another companion, or perhaps a volunteer caregiver from a local organization.)

• How does your parent like to be addressed (Mr., Miss, Mrs., Ms., first name)?

• How do you want the telephone answered? ("Hello!," or, "This is the Smith residence").

• Post emergency numbers by the phone, and provide a list of all important telephone numbers the companion should have handy. Include close family members, friends, your physician(s), pharmacy, hospital, and ambulance of choice. If 911 is not available in your area, include police and fire department numbers.

• The use of your telephone for the companion's private calls should be negotiated. How will long distance calls be paid for? How many personal calls will be permitted?

• Give instructions on particular chairs or seating arrangements your parent prefers and on items your parent likes to have at hand (telephone, tissues, wastebasket, water, pad and pencil, magazines, reading glasses, and so on).

• Does the companion have his or her own form of transportation that is reliable?

• Will a car be available for the companion's use, or is the companion to provide a car? How will car expenses be handled? Be sure that the companion shows you an up-to-date driver's license and insurance card before starting work.

• Will driving a car, aiding your parent through the appointment process, and filling pharmacy medications be expected? Make sure the companion knows where to take your parent, the value of arriving early enough not to rush and of making appointments during slow times of the day, and to be aware of any hunger and fatigue that may occur.

• If the companion will be driving your parent, is the automobile insurance adequate?

• Appliances, TV, and VCR equipment may need instructions for use. Provide this training for machines the companion will be expected to use and know.

• Medical, dental, and physical check-ups are routine for your parent. How much responsibility for these appointments will the companion be responsible for?

Meals

• What are preferred meal times?

• What are food requirements for each meal? Does your parent prefer a large meal mid-day or in the evening? What kinds of foods does your parent enjoy? Dislike?

• Are there any special preparations or instructions to be followed? What special diets need to be followed (such as low salt, low fat, or low sugar)?

• Are there any particular dishes, utensils, and cookware to be used? Not to be used?

• Clean-up instructions may include items that are not to be put in the dishwasher, pan surfaces that are not to be scratched, fragile glasses that need hand-wiping. Sets of special dishes may be off-limits for daily use.

Exercise and entertainment

• What exercise program should your parent begin or continue?

• Will the companion need to walk outdoors with your parent everyday, weather permitting?

• Are there any other activities planned?

• Continuing a social life, however limited, can be important to your parent. What will be continued (church functions, club meetings, luncheons with friends, day trips to see others, visitors for tea)? How much will the companion be involved in handling your parent's social life?

• Are there games or amusements your parent enjoys that the companion will participate in?

Grocery shopping

• Will grocery shopping be required of the companion? If so, how frequently and how far will he or she have to walk or drive?

• Do you prefer one particular grocery store for shopping? Specify brand names of items, if necessary. Do you expect coupons to be saved and used?

• How are groceries to be paid for (cash given to the companion, check made out to the store, charge account)?

Light housekeeping

• Make a list of expected light housekeeping duties and how often they must be performed. Most companions will not do heavy housekeeping but will assist with daily household chores.

• Give special instructions for use of products and cleaning method.

Laundry

• How frequently is laundry done?

• Provide instructions for clothing that requires special handling.

• Are some items to be sent out to a professional cleaner? If so, which, when, and how?

• Provide instructions on how clothing should be folded and where they should be put away.

Personal hygiene

• What is the procedure be for your parent's baths or showers? Aside from the companion being on the premises to prevent accidents, is other help needed? Should a bath schedule be encouraged as a routine?

• Does your parent need to be taken to a hairdresser or

barber? How often? Are appointments necessary, and should the companion make them?

Leaving your parent alone

• Determine how much time your parent needs to be alone. Many older people enjoy and need time by themselves; too much talking can tire them.

• Are short errands away from your parent permitted and safe?

• Can your parent spend the night alone?

• If changes in your parent's behavior, health, and mental alertness occur, to whom does the companion turn?

• If the companion must leave your employment for any period or terminate the work relationship, agree on some procedure (for example, two weeks' notice required) that will solve your parent's needs and avoid any risks. The companion must accept this commitment as part of the employment.

Evaluating nursing homes

The timing of the decision to place your parent in a nursing home is as individual as every person reading this book. Obviously, if you've determined care at home is not enough for your parent, you've skipped to this section. To reiterate, nursing home care is probably needed if:

• Health resources can't be adequately delivered in a home setting.

• Finances are limited. Expenses for home care can

be higher than for nursing home care. If your parent is eligible for Medicaid, this may be a good choice; most states won't pay for continued home-health care but will pay for nursing home care.

- Your parent requires a more secure setting than the home.

- You find yourself overwhelmed, both physically and emotionally, trying to fill in the gaps with the home-care arrangements you've made.

- A health care professional recommends nursing home care for your parent

For some elderly people, a time comes when remaining at home is no longer an option. If you find yourself having to screen and choose a nursing home, we offer questions to ask, items to be looked for, and issues to be addressed. Remember, you are a consumer prepared to spend good money to provide the best possible nursing home setting for your parent. It is worth your time and energy to investigate available nursing homes, and you will find differences among facilities. (For a detailed discussion of financing nursing home and other long-term care costs, see Chapter 5.)

Ask around. Talk to anyone you know and trust who has had experience with placing someone in a nursing home. But regardless of any recommendations, it is impossible to choose a home without actually visiting the institution and comparing your findings with other homes.

Nursing homes often have waiting lists for admission. Conduct your investigation early enough so that you don't feel caught needing an available bed. Settle on three to six choices and put your parent's name on the waiting lists of three. When making your rounds of local nursing homes, remember the administrator is a professional person, undoubtedly trying to run the best facility possible. For you, that means providing your parent with a positive, safe, and nurturing environment. The facility's administrator is potentially your ally, not an adversary.

Your first visit to any facility should be done by appointment, either with the administrator or the social worker responsible for admissions. You can learn a lot by looking, listening, and smelling. Most facilities will not make appointments for visits until after the morning-care routine is completed. Because food is so important, schedule your visit as close to mealtime as possible.

If after your visit you feel the home merits consideration as a finalist in your search, return unannounced, and have a second look around. Any facility that refuses to allow you entry without first making an appointment is not a place you'll want to seriously consider for your parent.

Whether you include your parent in your search depends on your situation. In most cases, your parent should make a visit after your list has been narrowed to one or two homes. Recognize that most elderly people resist nursing homes. If you have reached the conclusion that this is the best option given your situation, don't invite criticism from your parent that is aimed at nursing homes in general but against a specific choice. If you do, you'll be in a no-win situation. Nursing homes are not evil, last-effort choices.

They can be used for rehabilitation, short-term care following hospitalization, and some offer respite programs. They also provide skilled-nursing care with supportive therapies, such as physical therapy, speech therapy, and occupational therapy. For many people, this is the best and most appropriate choice. Watch for the following:

General information

• Are all licenses and certificates (for the facility, administrator, pharmacy, safety and health equipment, etc.) current and in order? Ask to see them; they are not private.

• What organization accredits the home?

• What are the visiting hours?

• What kind of in-service training is provided for the staff?

Overall appearance

• Are the grounds well maintained?

• Is there adequate parking for visitors?

• How are you greeted in the main reception area?

• Are the public areas and patients' rooms clean, bright, and cheerful?

• Are there any unpleasant odors?

• Is the noise level excessive?

• Are the fire doors clearly marked and closed?

• Is a Patient's Bill of Rights conspicuously posted?

Patient-care units

• Do people look well cared for? Do they look happy?

• Are patients up and around or in bed?

• Do patients seem to be sitting unattended for a long time?

• Are patients calling in vain for assistance? Or is the staff obvious and attentive?

• Is a patient's privacy respected or are doors open while treatment or assistance is being provided?

• How does the staff treat you? Are they open and able to answer your questions satisfactorily?

• Are there adequate safety provisions such as grab bars in the bathrooms, railings in the hallways, and non-slip floors in the patient areas?

Patient-care issues

• Will your parent's doctor visit in the home or will your parent have to be taken to the doctor's office?

• If your parent requires hospitalization, will his or her room be held for his or her return and for how long?

• What levels of care does the home provide?

• How does the staff handle wandering patients?

• Are restraints commonly used?

• Is daily exercise available for the patients?

• Is there an outdoors area for the patients?

• Is there a psychiatric consultant?

• Is a social worker available for both patients and family?

• Are services such as hairdresser or barber available?

• What types of recreational activities (outings, movies, etc.) are planned and how often?

Financing and logistics

- How are admissions determined? How long is the wait?
- What are the financial arrangements?
- Will a refund or partial refund be made if a patient chooses to leave and has prepaid the home?
- Can the home discharge a patient without the family's consent? If so, how much notice will be provided?
- Will the home accept Medicare or Medicaid payment?
- If a transfer to Medicaid is required, will the home await the payment without discharging the patient?
- How is spending money for the patients handled?
- Can personal items be brought from home? If so, which?
- Can a married couple room together?
- If only one parent is to be admitted, can the other visit and have a meal with the resident? Is there any charge?

Meals

- Are there any choices on the menu?
- How frequently does the menu repeat itself?
- Does the food look and smell appealing?
- Do the portions seem adequate?
- Are the meals well-balanced and offer variety?
- Do patients receive their trays while the food is still warm? If they need help eating, do they get it?
- Do people seem to be enjoying the meal or do they just push the food around on their plates?
- Can the food be prepared with varying consistencies such as semi-soft or pureed?

• Can the kitchen handle special food preferences or dietary restrictions? Is there a certified dietician on staff?

• Are there special meals prepared for birthdays, holidays, or other occasions?

• Is there any flexibility in the meal times?

• Are snacks and between-meal foods available? What kind?

• Is there any provision for refrigerated storage if food is brought in by family or friends?

Additional services

• Do dentists, podiatrists, and audiologists come to the facility to care for residents?

• Are the patients able to wear their own clothing?

• Are there provisions for the patient's personal laundry?

• Is the laundry done on the premises or sent out? Is there a problem with running short on linens? What happens to personal clothing? If no personal laundry can be done and you are unable to, will arrangements be made?

• Are clergy regularly involved with the patients? If so, what religions and in what manner?

• Is there a sundries store or some way for patients to purchase small, personal items?

Chapter 5

Paying for Care

M r. and Mrs. Spoletto, ages seventy-nine and seventy-four, respectively, came to our office with their children to discuss Mr. Spoletto's return home after a brief hospital stay and six-week rehabilitation period following a stroke. While Mr. Spoletto could speak, the left side of his body was paralyzed.

Like many older couples, he and his wife relied on their Social Security benefits plus a small monthly pension to pay their expenses. Mrs. Spoletto explained that the minimum home-health assistance they now received, two hours for three days a week, was insufficient to properly care for her husband. Unfortunately, their annual income placed them just above the Medicaid limits for financial assistance. Both were adamantly opposed to placing Mr. Spoletto in a nursing home. Their children were unable to either pay for his care or take their parents into their homes.

Since the Spolettos owned their home free and clear, we suggested the family look into a little-known program available to most older homeowners: the reverse annuity mortgage.

Homeowners are allowed to borrow money against the equity in their homes, receiving a monthly cash distribution. The loan plus interest is paid when the house is sold.

Based on the additional number of hours of care Mr. Spoletto required, we figured he and his wife needed an additional $1,200 per month. Initially hesitant about tapping into their home's equity and diminishing their children's inheritance, they decided, with their children's encouragement, to file the necessary papers.

This plan allowed Mr. Spoletto to live in his own home until his death two years later.

Demystifying Medicare

Relax. Take a deep breath. The puzzling, murky world of paying for care is not as confusing as it now appears. At each step along the way you can find assistance, direction, and advice. Discharge planners at the hospital will tell you what is and isn't covered. Nursing-home admissions coordinators will review finances with you, file for Medicare coverage, and assist you in filing for Medicaid if appropriate. Elder-law specialists, private case managers, or geriatric assessment center staffs can and will provide financial direction as well. Part Three of this book lists national organizations that will be able provide counsel and assistance in working through the maze of paying for care. Two large national organizations are especially helpful: The National Association of Private Geriatric Care Managers and the National Academy of Elder Law Attorneys.

In Chapter 3 we highlighted the types of eldercare

available and approximate costs for each. Depending on specific medical needs, expenses can run from $7.50 per hour for a companion to $36,000 per year or more for a bed in a skilled-nursing facility. Especially for facilities, there are sets of rules and regulations for payment, and some standards are now set state by state. They should be reviewed, often with an attorney or accountant, to fully understand what you're getting into.

Most people assume that Medicare foots most of these bills. In fact, Medicare pays very little of home care or nursing-home care expenses. In this country today, about 55 percent of nursing-home care (intermediate and skilled) is paid by the patients themselves. About 40 percent is paid by Medicaid (sometimes referred to as Title XIX, the federal act that established this government program), and about 2 to 3 percent is paid by Medicare.

To qualify for Medicare reimbursement of these services, an individual must spend at least three days (seventy-two hours) in the hospital and be eligible for rehabilitation. Medicare will then pay all of the nursing home bill for up to one hundred days of care, provided the patient shows improvement with rehabilitative treatment. For example, if mom falls and breaks her hip, she can receive assistance at home, including home-health aides, nursing supervision and in-home physical therapy. Medicare will continue to pay these costs until she is either functioning on her own or has plateaued and no longer shows signs of improvement.

However, regardless of improvement or current status of condition, Medicare will only pay for one hundred days of treatment and services per calendar year. This holds true if the patient must be re-hospitalized for another condition, or even if another medical emergency presents itself. Medicare pays up to one hundred days per patient, per year, period. (Medicaid [called Medical in California] kicks in at this point, but only if a person is essentially impoverished. See below.)

You're no doubt thinking, "If Medicare will pay for home rehabilitation too, why even consider a nursing home?" The answer is that Medicare may determine that the rehabilitative needs of the patient require only twelve to fifteen hours a week of a home-health aide, once-weekly visits by a physical therapist, plus a nurse visit once or perhaps twice a week. You may think this is inadequate, and of course you can opt to pay for more care yourself. But you have no say in the care Medicare authorizes and will pay for.

Again, the majority of home care and nursing home expenses are paid privately. This can be an extremely expensive undertaking. Too often failure on the part of the elderly to anticipate or plan for their retirement years places an especially heavy burden on the well spouse when catastrophic medical problems arise. The retired seventy-five-year old couple living on a pension and Social Security income of $2,000 per month, which seemed adequate as long as both were reasonably healthy, quickly finds that it is eaten up in no time by health-care service providers, medication, and doctor's bills.

Let's look at a specific example. Mr. and Mrs. Clark fit the above description. One day, Mr. Clark suffers a stroke leaving him with speech difficulties and unable to walk. A rehabilitation setting accepts him as a patient. After six weeks, however, he no longer shows improvement. Medicare will no longer pay for continued inpatient care and he must be discharged from the facility. If he is able to return home, Mrs. Clark will certainly need assistance to dress and bathe him. Their monthly $2,000 is not enough to cover the costs. A home-health aide for four hours a day, five days a week will run $350 per week or $1,400 per month. Similarly, nursing-home care can cost $3,000 to $5,000 per month. The couple will need to use their savings, IRAs, CDs, and so on to cover the costs of care, regardless of where that care is provided.

The benefits of a
reverse annuity mortgage

But there are other options when there are little or no savings to draw on. Consider the **reverse annuity mortgage.** This functions much like a home equity loan, tapping into the user's real estate equity. If Mr. and Mrs. Jones own their home, say with a value of $150,000, a bank may loan them up to 70 percent of the equity in the home (or $105,000, assuming the home is owned free and clear), paid out in monthly installments to meet their expenses. The bank recoups the loan, plus interest, when the house is sold. This approach can free up a more-than adequate supply of capital to cover the costs of keeping Mr. Jones at home while not impoverishing Mrs. Jones. This option becomes even more attractive when there is only one living parent in need of care. By using the reverse annuity mortgage, a patient gets the care he or she needs while still remaining in the home.

Another rapidly accessible source for needed cash is cashing in on life insurance policies. Recently, AARP (American Association of Retired Persons), through its insurance underwriter, offered its life insurance subscribers the option, at no cost, to be able to cash in their policies at any time if severe medical problems or care needs arise. Surprisingly, less than 10 percent of the policy holders chose to exercise the option. The reason is unclear, but presumably many view life insurance as an inheritance for their survivors, and people don't seem to want to think of using that money to pay for the cost of care for themselves. But it is an option people can and should consider.

Long-term care insurance

In the last two or three years, **long-term care insurance** has emerged as an important safeguard against medical disability. However, there is a lot of confusion about what these policies really do and whether they are financially worthwhile and fiscally prudent. Federal guidelines have recently been enacted to protect consumers. They are not good options if one has an immediate need for care, for like all health insurance policies, they have immediate-use prohibitions. They should be considered as part of an overall insurance portfolio. Basic long-term care insurance pays for nursing-home or home-health care for the policy holder. Like other types of insurance, it pays a daily fixed amount (for example, $100 per day as long as required for either home-health or nursing-home care), full payment for a specific period of time (coverage for the complete cost of care for either thirty, ninety, or one hundred and eighty days), or a daily fixed amount until the full-benefit limit of the policy is reached (for example, $100 per day with a maximum payout of $25,000).

To bring long-term care insurance into clearer perspective, only one out of one thousand people will ever need the insurance benefits of his or her homeowner's policy, one out of one hundred will need the benefits of auto insurance, but one out of five will eventually require the cash benefits from long-term care insurance. Yet it remains the least purchased of all insurance policies.

It is beyond the scope of this chapter to examine the range of long-term care policies available. Talk to your or your parent's insurance agent. You'll also want to discuss who should purchase the insurance. Should children buy a policy for their parents, to ensure peace of mind as well as protection of assets? Or should the elderly with adequate financial resources purchase coverage for themselves? Long-term care insurance makes less sense for widowed individuals with limited assets because most, if not all, states have laws that prohibit the denial of admission to long-term care facilities based on the ability to pay. Medicaid will pay for long-term care for individuals who meet the financial requirements (see below).

Dependent care pre-taxed dollars

Thanks to recent federal tax regulations, many companies offer employees the opportunity to take pre-tax payroll dollars and set them aside for dependant care or related health care expenses. The program allows employees to estimate their annual medical expenses and deduct a fixed amount of money from each paycheck, which is not subject to federal, state, or local income taxes. (Social Security is not withheld from these dollars, nor is this amount included in your total Social Security obligation.) Parents with young children in daycare will often have the monthly daycare costs drawn directly from their paychecks in this manner to cover these costs. (For example, if the daycare center costs $100 per week, the $5,200 set aside from their paycheck will not only pay the center, but will also reduce their taxable annual income by the same $5,200.)

This approach can be utilized to cover costs for the care of dependent parents as well. The downside is that if you overestimate the amount of money you will need, the company withholding the pre-tax dollars gets to keep the unused portion at the end of the year. In addition, the maximum amount of pre-tax dollars that can be withheld varies by state. Ask your employer if it offers this program. As a rule of thumb, any health care-related expense that would normally be an allowable deduction on your IRS form is eligible, including eyeglasses, hearing aides, medications, doctors' bills, as well as home-health care and nursing-home expenses.

The ABCs of Medicaid

The last source of payment for services is Medicaid (Medi-cal in California). Enacted as Title XIX of the Social Security Act, this government program pays for health care services for those who meet its eligibility requirements. The hard truth is that one needs to be impoverished to be eligible for Medicaid.

Financial eligibility for Medicaid is based on whether an applicant's resources are below an amount set by each state. To determine the amount in your state (or the state where your parent resides), you can:

- Contact the state office that administers Medicaid

- Contact the social work staff at a community hospital

- Contact the state's Department of Aging

- Consult an elder-law attorney

Nineteen states have not adopted the "medically needy" option for their Medicaid program. In these states, individuals whose income exceeds limits set by the state do not qualify for Title XIX assistance. In 1992, the income limitation in most of these states was $1,266 per month for an individual, $2,532 for a couple. This means that if the combined monthly income from Social Security, pensions, IRAs, Keoghs, and so on exceeds these amounts, eligibility is denied.

In other states, the question concerns assets (which

could be used to pay for medical expenses) rather than income. Again, each state sets its own asset cap. In Colorado it's $2,000, in Connecticut $2,600, in New York $3,050. Many states also allow for a burial allowance, which is not factored into the cap. In these states, once an individual has spent all assets except $3,050 (in New York), they are eligible for Medicaid. In most states, certain assets are exempt from the calculation of the cap:

- The individual's home (referred to as the homestead)

- Essential personal property (clothing, furnishings)

- Automobile

- Limited life insurance (if the face value of the policy is $1,500 or less, the cash value is exempt even if it exceeds $1,500)

There are, not surprisingly, some stipulations to consider. The home must be the primary residence of the individual and is exempt from asset determination only if the healthy spouse continues to live in it or the couple has an adult dependent child who lives in the home (dependent refers to a child older than twenty-one who is either blind or disabled or to a child younger than twenty-one). Also, if a sibling with an equity interest in the house has resided there for a minimum of one year prior to the applicant's application, it is likewise exempt from asset determination. Finally, the home is also exempt if it is the residence of a son or daughter of the individual who had also lived in the home for a minimum of two years prior to their parent's institutionalization and who had provided care for the parent, thus enabling the patient to remain at home for a time.

It is estimated that 85 percent of widowed and single American women older than seventy-five meet eligibility requirements for Medicaid. Those who don't and who require nursing-home care will, on average, meet eligibility requirements after thirteen weeks (the approximate time it takes them to go through their assets). Couples who require nursing-home care will spend their assets and meet eligibility requirements in six months.

In formulating new Medicaid laws, Congress was aware of the hardship imposed on many spouses of institutionalized patients who were left without adequate income because of nursing-home costs. The current law deals with this problem by requiring states to pay monthly income allowances to the at-home spouse in amounts of at least $985 plus an excess shelter allowance (if shelter costs exceed 25 percent of the basic allotted income or a flat amount of $1,718 per month. New York has adopted the full $1,718 allowance for at-home spouses).

Support suits can still be brought on behalf of at-home spouses if the state's income allowance is proven to be insufficient in a particular case. In some cases, a fair hearing may be an appropriate remedy. To fully understand and assess eligibility, consultation with an attorney is often necessary and extremely helpful.

The basics of Medigap

Medicare Supplemental Insurance (Medigap) is yet another option that many Medicare-eligible individuals fail to purchase. As of January 1992, all policies have to conform to one of ten standards outlined by the federal government. One gap policy is all anyone ever needs, because only one will pay. The typical "little old lady scam" of selling multiple policies to cover "everything" is just that—a scam. (Check *Consumer Reports* for an evaluation of these policies and the ten standards developed by the National Association of Insurance Commissioners.) Policies can cover the co-insurance portion of the bill (after Medicare pays 80 percent) to everything that isn't put applicable to Medicare. These policies do not, however, cover nursing-home expenses.

The federal government has recently published a free booklet, "Guide to Health Insurance for People with Medicare." Write to the Consumer Information Center, Department 515-Z, Pueblo, Colorado, 81009.

Medicare is divided into Part A (hospital care) and Part B (outpatient costs and doctors' fees). Part A covers a hospital stay of up to a specified number of days in full, after a deductible is paid, and covers additional days in decreasing amounts. A limited period of skilled-nursing care may be available if it is immediately preceded by a hospital stay and considered by Medicare to be a continuation of hospital care. Part B covers a portion of physician and certain other medical services as determined by Medicare, with the patient having to pay the balance. Some physicians do accept Medicare patients on assignment, which means they accept the payment as set by Medicare and do not look for any additional payment beyond the patient's co-payment, usually 20 percent of the bill.

You can obtain listings of physicians who will accept such assignments from a local Social Security office. The local county medical society may also offer this information. Coverage for Medicare Parts A and B is obtained by filing an application at a patient's local Social Security office a minimum of four months prior to retirement at age sixty-five or later. Part B requires a premium which is withheld from the monthly Social Security check.

Medigap plans provide a core set of benefits. These include annual deductibles and co-payments:

- For nursing home stay Medicare pays 100 percent for the first 20 days, then approximately 80 percent for the following 80 days; Medigap will make up the difference

- The co-insurance (the portion the patient must pay) amount of 61 to 90 hospitalization days

- The co-insurance amount for 60 non-renewable, lifetime hospital inpatient reserve days

- For hospital charges that otherwise would have been paid by Medicare, after all Medicare hospital benefits are exhausted (up to 365 days)

- Part B co-insurance (20 percent) once the annual deductible (currently $100) has been paid

Some Medigap plans provide one or more additional benefits. The more benefits offered, the more expensive the plan. Additional options include:

- A $625 Part A deductible
- Co-insurance amount for the 21st through 100th day of skilled-nursing care
- Part B deductible
- Certain benefits for at-home recovery services
- Outpatient prescription drugs

More elaborate plans may include:

- Intermediate or custodial care given at home by a home-health agency

Traditional health care insurance companies (Blue Cross, Blue Shield, Travellers, Prudential, etc.) offer reams of information on a range of Medigap plans that are easy to understand and even easier to purchase. It is money well spent if you know what your parent's needs are. It makes a nice birthday, anniversary, or holiday gift. You can arrange to pay the quarterly premiums on a gap policy for them.

Chapter 6

Legal Issues and Financial Planning

M r. and Mrs. Vincent had been married for forty-three years. He was a graphic artist, she a school teacher. She and her husband had led a very active, financially successful life together, acquiring a magnificent home and a number of retirement accounts. They came to our clinic after an initial examination by their local neurologist. Mr. Vincent was suffering from Alzheimer's disease. Mrs. Vincent had been advised by her family and attorneys on several occasions to protect her finances, as her husband would likely require skilled-nursing care in the future. But Mrs. Vincent had been slow to take action.

Her inability to move forward and do some serious financial planning was caused by a fear that taking the necessary steps to ensure her own financial well-being would hasten his decline. As is so often the case, bad consequences occurred through inaction. Mr Vincent was hospitalized for pneumonia and suffered a severe deterioration in his overall functioning. His wife was incapable of providing the intensive care and assistance he now required.

Because their retirement accounts and assets were jointly held, she was facing significant, out-of-pocket costs to provide nursing-home care for her husband. On the advice of the couple's attorney and after much emotional upheaval, Mrs. Vincent not only agreed to place her husband in a nursing home but reluctantly agreed to file for divorce in a last-ditch attempt to secure some small piece of the financial assets for her own later years.

The importance of financial planning, especially if one is faced with a chronic, debilitating disease like Alzheimer's disease, can't be overstated. Mrs. Vincent's only option was also the most difficult emotionally: divorcing her husband to try and protect her assets.

In keeping with our recommendation that you search out experts in geriatric care (internists, psychiatrists, social workers, case managers, and so on), we urge you not to overlook expert help with legal and financial issues as well.

While this chapter will highlight a number of basic health care-related documents, legal counsel is necessary to guarantee that the information you receive, documents you complete, and financial planning and management you put in place will all be appropriate and within the guidelines established by federal and state law.

This chapter will also highlight the federal regulations on what are referred to as advanced-life directives, commonly known as living wills. And, we'll address health care agents, durable power of attorney for health care directives (commonly referred to as health care proxies), conservator-ship, and basic financial planning.

Each state has developed its own standards for these matters; be sure to familiarize yourself with the rules and regulations of your state or the state in which your parent resides. To assume that legal documents are easily trans-ferrable from one state to the next is an error that can cause you and your parent unnecessary emotional and financial pain. Our goal is to acquaint you with the type of legal documents that exist, what they mean, and how they can help make future decision-making easier.

Advanced-life directives (living wills)

Advanced-life directives became federal law in October 1991. Their goal is to allow competent individuals to de-cree the type of care they want if they become incapable of deciding themselves. Often referred to as "death with dignity" procedures, advanced-life directives allow an individual to stipulate whether they want to be put on a ventilator, have cardio-pulmonary resuscitation per-formed in the event of cardiac arrest, be given food and fluids through a feeding tube, or have their life sustained by mechanical means. An advanced-life directive takes the burden of decision-making off the family and provides a legal means to family and physicians treating that indi-vidual of knowing how the patient would manage their own care. It allows the medical profession to "pull the plug," to turn off all mechanical life-support equipment when there is little or no chance that the patient will recover their normal existence.

People assume that living wills are only for eighty-year-olds, yet every major court decision regarding the wishes of a comatose patient was made for a young, vital individual, the most famous being the Supreme Court's Cruzan decision, made on behalf of a twenty-six-year old woman who suffered a catastrophic accident.

Most people believe they must have a written, signed, and notarized document to constitute a proper living will, but the truth is much simpler. At the very least, a discussion about future decisions must occur; take notes and document this discussion. If such a discussion hasn't taken place and a family wants life-support machines turned off, they may need to petition a court to get legal authority to make decisions. It's best to plan ahead if possible. Standard living-will forms are available from every health care institution, and can and should be reviewed with everyone who might be involved before being signed and witnessed.

Health care agents

A competent individual may legally appoint another individual to make health care decisions for them if they cannot. The agent is given legal authority to consent to or withhold treatment. Often the individual appointed is a spouse, child, or close personal friend. The agent only becomes effective when physicians deem a patient incapable of making reasonable decisions on his or her own behalf.

Durable power of attorney for health care (health care proxies) and conservatorships

A durable power of attorney is a way to appoint an individual who has the legal right to manage one's finances (a living will or health care proxy give no legal authority to another to manage an individual's finances, pay bills, write checks, or dispose of assets to pay bills). Too often a parent (often the sole surviving parent) has not made any arrangements to allow their children, an attorney, or a close family friend access to their financial assets for the purposes of paying bills, filing income taxes, or managing their affairs.

The only legal alternative to appointing someone ahead of time is the lengthy and often expensive route of filing for conservatorship in probate court. The onus is on the applicant to show that the individual is incapable of managing their own finances (or incapable of making medical decisions). The court then has the legal authority to appoint someone to act for the individual. It is not unusual for the conservatorship process to take a number of weeks, with a cost ranging up to $2,500.

The more you can anticipate and plan for the future, the easier it will be to manage, and the more likely your or your parent's wishes will be carried out.

Estate planning

In a perfect world, you would be able to skip over this portion of the chapter. You and your parents would have met with their attorney and accountant and established the necessary trusts, transfer of assets, gifts, and so on to maximize holding on to assets and minimizing tax liabilities. In reality, people are remarkably naive about inheritance taxes, the tax benefits of annual gifts, and similar procedures. All too often, it is only when a parent has been diagnosed with Alzheimer's disease that the spouse and family are suddenly forced to begin to address these issues.

Estate planning is a specialty unto itself. Our advice is simple: Concern yourself with the long-term financial well-being of both the ill and the at-home spouse, as well as the rest of the family. Failure to respond to this need can prove to be quite costly, both financially and emotionally. Elder-law attorneys, tax advisors, and estate planners can begin the work of assisting you and your parents to ensure their financial health.

If you haven't yet dealt with these issues, do so at the earliest possible opportunity. We encourage you to find the courage to address the situation today.

Part II

Coping

Chapter 7

Parents

In addition to managing the care of your parent, you have to cope with the trauma that goes along with it. This is true for those who are providing hands-on care as well as for those who are supervising and coordinating that care. In the next six chapters we'll focus on the emotional issues that come into play for those caring for a parent.

We'll look at your interaction with your parents, siblings, children, spouse, and employer. How do you respond when your sibling says, "Mom always liked you best. You take care of her and leave me out of it"? What do you do when your spouse and children tell you they don't want your parent coming to live with them because it will take too much of your time and attention? How do you deal with an employer who is only concerned with the bottom line and doesn't care about your aging parent? We'll explore these issues, and show you how to forge a care consensus with other family members for the benefit of everyone. We'll also examine how you can best deal with yourself—your own concerns, guilt, and fears.

Parents first

The most critical party in the entire care equation is your parents themselves—not just tending to their physical needs, but providing them with the emotional support they require as well. Often, it is coping with these emotional needs that is most time consuming and stressful. Adult children faced with caring for an elderly parent most often ask, "How do I talk to my parents about..." anything and everything: their illness, their medical care, their need for rehabilitation or nursing care, why mom can't stay in her home anymore, why dad can't live by himself, and so on.

No one likes to be the bearer of bad news. No one enjoys having to make decisions for others, especially if negative consequences may occur. No one wants to be thought of as imposing their will on those they love. But sometimes we have to. Of course, what you say and how you say it will vary, depending on the mental and physical state of your parent. So, how do you talk to your parents about...? If you're like most people, probably not easily. If however, you start from a base of love, understanding, and compassion, the task will be much less complicated. Remember, your job is to help your parent, not *be* their parent. Most often, what that means is not making decisions for them but helping them to make informed, reasonable decisions for themselves.

Respect your parents' judgment

If your parent is physically ill but mentally capable, then you cannot make arbitrary decisions for them. At no point do you have the right to say, "It's just as well if...," "Why put her through this...," "At her age, why bother...." Look at the situation another way. The U.S. Constitution declares that the government cannot deprive someone of life, liberty, or property without due process. Don't take it upon yourself to deny your parent that which the government can't.

How do you know if you are being too overbearing in the decision-making process? Use the Me Rule again. How would you react if your child were making the same decisions for you that you're making for your parent? Would you be pleased or dismayed? Whatever the answer, you can safely assume that your parent would feel the same way. Of course, if it is not possible for your parent to make informed, rational decisions, then you and your family must make those decisions for them.

Realize that your parent may be frightened, and with good reason. The prospect of pain, of suffering, of institutional loneliness scares most people. It is this fear that needs to be addressed. The only way to do that is to sit down and talk about it. When is the best time to have such a talk? There is no such time. Assuredly, this is not a conversation that should take place at 4 p.m. after the Thanksgiving meal, in front of the television, or during the halftime of a football game. This is a conversation that needs to take place with all the family present, at a time clearly set up to discuss this issue. (Maybe the Saturday after Thanksgiving.)

If you're like most people, this conversation has never taken place. And if you now find yourself in the middle of an acute medical crisis, the issues are greater and the emotional burden you and your family have to bear is much heavier. But face it: Everyone is afraid of being in the hospital and not knowing what's going to happen to them. If your parent is elderly, everything now seems life-threatening, and so that fear is compounded.

The first thing you'll probably have to deal with after mom's hospitalization is her fear of not knowing what she's been admitted for, what's really wrong with her, and what the future may hold for her. If she's been hospitalized for something straightforward (such as a hip fracture), dealing with these fear issues is much simpler. What, however, do you do if mom's medical case is far more complicated or confusing? How much should you tell her? How much does she really need to know at any given moment?

Too often, adult children decide the information will be overwhelming for mom or dad and say little or nothing, but this is grossly unfair. It's patronizing to treat your parents like children. Out of a misplaced sense of concern and love, the family has placed themselves in the position of knowing what is best for their parent. This is what

Dr. Robert Butler, first director of the National Institute on Aging, referred to as ageism, a bias based solely on the age of a person. It permeates the medical establishment, which reflects the ageism that exists in our culture. Youth, beauty, and vigor are valued. Because silver-haired, little old women and men represent none of these attributes, three very important things don't happen:

- A frank discussion about what mom would want done for herself never takes place.

- If she has a life-threatening illness, her need to get her affairs in order, take stock and reflect back on her life, or make plans for her death, is never satisfied.

- The family minimizes her emotional state and the impact that this as yet unmentioned illness will have on her.

In addition, you may fail to appreciate that to the extent your parent is capable and willing to make these decisions herself (even if you don't agree with it), the more you and your family will be able to reduce the sense of responsibility and guilt. This is true especially if a negative outcome occurs. In the end, it will be her decision, not yours, if you have the respect to allow her to make it.

First things first: You have to get through the immediate crisis, if you're in one. Say it becomes clear from surgery that rehabilitation will be necessary for your parent. Rehabilitation isn't just physical therapy; it often requires ongoing medication and nursing care to return the patient to his or her greatest level of functioning. As mom is starting to recover from the surgery and look better and feel better, the sooner you can discuss what happens next, the better. Be clear and direct: "Mom, you're not going to be able to return to your apartment immediately. It doesn't seem to make sense to have you come home with me when we can't provide the nursing care that you're going to need. What we're going to do is make arrangements for you to have a short rehabilitative stay in a nursing home, anywhere from four to twelve weeks. After that, we'll see about getting you home again." Don't give the impression that mom is being sent to the nursing home with no plan of going home. The nursing home is to be viewed as an interim stay for purposes of rehabilitation to facilitate getting home. That always has to be the goal.

Let's say, though, that the reason for mom's hospitalization is that she's suffered a stroke. She is now so impaired that it's going to be impossible for her to manage at home, even with home-health services. You need to let her know that she's going to a nursing home because it's the only thing that makes sense at this point. But be sure you still hold out the hope that there is a possibility of rehabilitation.

Of course, the reality is that if, after three months of acute care in the nursing home, mom still hasn't made any progress, she's not going to make it in six months or nine months or a year. Realistically, it's just not going to happen. This will precipitate a very understandable grief on the part of both mom and the family.

But cross that bridge if and when it comes. Deal with each issue as it presents itself. Don't try to make assumptions or pronouncements when you don't know what the long-term reality will be. Why scare mom or yourself needlessly?

When parents have to be apart

Sometimes the situation is this: Mom's sick and needs nursing-home care, and dad does not. Again, the problem is usually not as great as it sounds, especially if the separation is only for the relatively brief rehabilitation period.

Our experience tells us that the only time spouses are separated is when one has a diagnosis of dementia and is no longer able to manage at home. By this time, all attempts to use community-based resources have been exhausted. Mom needs to be admitted to a nursing home because she is loud, combative, paranoid, incontinent, and struggling with caregivers. Dad is overwhelmed, distraught, depressed, and incapable of managing the situation. Often, placement in a nursing home, especially one in the community where mom and dad live, is not as big a struggle as you might imagine. For one, it's a relief for dad, who, after three to six months, is able to readjust his life to visiting mom in a nursing home every day, every other day, or twice a week, and have a life of his own.

A bigger difficulty comes when dad wants to join mom in the nursing home. From the nursing home's point of view, the needs of a couple are remarkably different from the needs of an ill individual. Most facilities won't keep a couple together. So, how do you manage this situation, when your parents just don't want to be alone? Try to convey to dad the reality a relatively healthy person faces in an environment where, except for the staff, everybody is ill but you. That can be tremendously depressing, unless the facility is mixed, with both skilled and intermediate-level care.

However, many nursing homes have a mixed population, with many patients who are reasonably physically sound. If this is the case, there's often plenty for the healthy spouse to do. Keep in mind that this usually becomes an issue not when your parents are in their sixties but when mom is eighty-three and dad is eighty-six and frail but otherwise functioning fine. If the nursing home is one with mixed levels of care, the solution can work out well, since physical-care demands are now the responsibility of the nursing-home staff.

Consider the cost, though: It's incredibly expensive for two people to live in a nursing home, perhaps $6,000 to 7,000 a month. Medicaid may be the answer. If dad has a clearly defined need to be in a nursing home, and again, he and mom have very limited resources (see Chapter 5), then Medicaid will cover it. Remember that if dad doesn't really need the care provided by a nursing home, then by law he can't be admitted, even if you or he can afford to pay for it.

Federal law clearly states that all patients who are seeking admission to a nursing home must go through what is known as a Level I screening by a state-contracted agency, often the department of income maintenance, which administers Medicaid. (Who pays is not a factor. In theory, and in law, it should be, and we expect a suit will eventually be brought to challenge this stricture.)

Often the healthy spouse moves in with the children. Younger elders, those sixty-five to seventy-four, will continue to reside in their senior housing unit, their apartment, or their own home; they still drive, provide their own transportation, and visit their spouse every day. Often the nursing-home visits become their main social activity. Surviving spouses often remain as volunteers after their mates have died.

How to respond when you and your parent disagree

Imagine you say, "Dad, come and live with us; we'll make arrangements for your therapy," but dad says, "I don't want to live with you; I don't want to be a burden. Just send me to a home where I can get back on my own two feet." At bottom the issue here is, who's in charge? How do you cope with the parent who is unwilling to consider the plan everyone else agrees is the course of action to be taken? Dad, rightly or wrongly, wants to have the final decision-making responsibility. Is his request to go to a nursing home unreasonable? Or is it that this decision makes you feel guilty, that you're not doing enough for him?

You need to be able to step back and assess the entire picture. Your parent may feel less that he is being sloughed off to some facility if it is the doctor pointing out the choices that are appropriate for care. If you include everyone in the family up front, including dad, and let them be part of the process instead of saying, "It's this facility" or

"Here's where you're going, period," your parent won't feel so resentful.

The reverse may also arise. Is it unreasonable for dad, who has been hospitalized and now needs more care, to want to come to your home for a month for rehabilitation? If you and your spouse work, how can you manage this? But maybe you can work it out, instead of rushing into the simple solution of a nursing home. Remember, options exist with just about any situation. Examine all of them before making any decision. Your purpose is not to get your parents to do what you want but to consider what's really best for them.

Sometimes, though, only one option exists. Dad's medical needs require him to enter a facility, but he is adamantly opposed to the idea. What do you do? The whole issue is emotionally charged. You need to understand that often your parent's initial response is a result of fears of despair, distrust, disillusion, and abandonment. You will do your research and find the best facility you can for your parent. After a three- to five-week adjustment period, you'll find out that dad's initial hostile and withdrawn response has abated. Be sure you give your parent—and yourself—this adjustment time before taking your parent out. If everyone responded to initial dislikes, then few children would ever make it past the first four days of kindergarten! Most good consulting psychiatrists don't treat such emotion as depression; rather, it's adjustment. For your parent, it's a major life crisis, right on the heels of being sick and hospitalized, another major life crisis.

Remember: keep everything in perspective—for you, for your parent, for everyone involved.

Take a common example that often comes up. You've determined that dad, who has always prized himself on his driving, shouldn't be behind the wheel any longer. Dad's had more than three accidents, he gets lost, but the '64 Pontiac is his pride and joy. How do you deal with this? The doctor may play the role of "bad guy" for the family, or maybe one of the following scenarios will help you out:

- A grandson desperately needs a car for work or college. He can't afford it, but maybe grandpa can help out.

- Consider hiding the keys, or disable the car. How do you disable the car? Ask your local mechanic to remove the ground to the battery. The car won't start.

Other family members may object. They argue that dad only drives to church. He hasn't been lost or had any accidents. Though mom is clearly anxious, they refuse to discuss taking the car away from dad. Consider hiring a driver. Try the local retirement volunteer corps or similar service.

The point is to reach an agreement everyone can live with.

Chapter 8

Siblings

$\mathcal{E}$arlier in this book we stressed the importance of involving other family members in decisions about your parents' care. Unless you are an only child, you'll most likely deal with your siblings. But what happens if your relationships with your siblings are not the greatest? Problems with sibling rivalry may go back as many as twenty, thirty, or more years. Often a family crisis exposes friction between family members. Despite the pressure to cave in to these emotional problems, don't lose sight of what's really at stake—the health and care of your parent.

Here are some examples of what often happens:

• The oldest female child (though not necessarily the oldest child) who lives closest to mom or dad is, by default, responsible. In the case of an only child, or if the nearest child happens to be a son, then it's often his wife to whom the burden and responsibility falls.

• If mom or dad gave you something substantial, such as a large sum of money or the family business, you are often made to feel responsible for their care and can't shirk that responsibility to your siblings.

• If you're busy, you may feel you don't have to take a role in helping to care for your parent.

• Siblings may minimize or otherwise undermine the decisions made by the sibling who has assumed responsibility.

• A sibling who makes unilateral decisions that are "in the best interest of mom or dad" guarantees family conflict.

Try to keep these points in mind:

• Regardless of whether you honestly feel you know what to do, you have to do something.

• Often the solution to a problem is right under your nose if you don't let sibling struggles keep you from seeing appropriate choices.

• If you are too far away or too busy to take a primary role in your parent's care, you have no voice in criticizing the ultimate decisions that are made by those providing the care.

A particularly painful case of sibling turmoil involved a thirty-two-year-old woman we'll call Alice. Alice's mom, a widow, was diagnosed with Alzheimer's disease. Alice had two sisters and a younger brother, all in their early to late thirties. Alice was unmarried, unlike her siblings.

After discussions with her siblings, she elected to quit her lucrative job and move back home to take care of mom.

Although the house was owned by mom and her Social Security check put food on the table and paid taxes and utilities, Alice's siblings agreed to pay her $1,000 a month, $333 each, to compensate her for giving up her career and to provide her with some income. In addition, they agreed to each take a turn caring for mom so Alice could have three weeks of vacation a year.

For two years this arrangement continued successfully. Then, about five weeks after her mom's last visit, Alice called to say she had to bring mom in immediately. We found no change for the worse in her mother's condition, but when we sat and talked with a sobbing Alice, we began to understand what had prompted this episode. Mom had walked into the kitchen, and asked, "Who are you? What are you doing in my house?" Alice, understanding a fair amount about her mother's illness, tried to reassure her.

"Mom, it's me, Alice."

"Alice, who's Alice? Where's Jack?"

"Jack's married, living in Seattle."

"What are you talking about? Jack's not married. Jack's at baseball practice."

Jack was sixteen years old in her mother's mind. Alice, who had moved home to prove to her mom that though neglected as a child was in fact "the good daughter," was suddenly confronted with all of her own feelings of inadequacy. Not only didn't her mother know who she was, she didn't care.

The structure that had seemingly worked so well in satisfying everybody's needs for two years fell apart overnight. All Alice wanted was out. Unfortunately, no one saw this coming. Her brother and sisters never bothered to say, "Why is our single sister willing to give up her career and social life to return home and take care of Mom?" It answered their needs and took them off the hook in terms of having to provide care for mom. It resolved their conflict and thus no one, at that point, looked at other issues that needed addressing.

Communication is key

We urge you to discuss the issue early on. Everyone's got to be open and fair and look at the reality of the situation. If sister A renovates her downstairs den into a kind of apartment for mom, what are the responsibilities of brother B and sister C? Though for each family the specifics will be unique, it has to be a discussion that takes place with the family. Often parents, unless they're still living in their own home, don't have any resources aside from their Social Security checks. Some parents offer to pay their children a fair rent out of their Social Security funds, since they may pay the same amount in a senior housing arrangement anyway. Sometimes, when parents still live in their own home, they'll use the assets generated through the sale of their home to renovate the child's home for their own use. While this increases the value of and net worth of the child's house, the child is not being compensated for providing care.

In spite of this, one sibling will often raise this seeming inequity as an issue. "Why should you get $50,000 to renovate your house?" The simple answer is, "You take the $50,000, renovate your house, and you take care of mom." Usually, that's the end of the discussion.

Though that may seem somewhat abrupt, the bottom-line goal isn't diplomacy, it's honesty. If these issues are not discussed, they become problems later on. Talk about the issues, get past the crisis of the moment, and move forward together.

Chapter 9

Spouse

There is no denying that eldercare, like many other responsibilities, puts a strain on a marriage. As with any crisis, however, love, understanding, compassion, and just plain courtesy can mitigate a potentially devastating situation. A marriage can actually be strengthened through shared and conquered adversity. In this chapter we will show you how to make your partner an ally, and how to make time for each other in spite of the time required to attend to a crisis. It is possible to be a good mate as well as a good child.

Assuming both you and your spouse are reasonably caring, understanding, and sensible people, this relationship should be the easiest to handle, certainly easier than asking mom about her thoughts about a living will or deciding where to move dad for extended treatment. Ideally, before you and your spouse are in the midst of an acute situation, you'll have sat down and discussed this in much the same way you've discussed any number of other issues throughout your lives together. The answer to the question, "How are we going to handle this issue with my (or your) parent?" may not be simple or easily resolved, but it should be manageable and will depend a great deal on your own resources—emotional, financial, and logistical.

It is unfair, however, to assume that what is good for the goose will not be good for the gander. It is fairly common to find that one partner in the marriage either has no need to provide care for his or her parents while the spouse does. Or, that one partner is an only child while the other comes from a large family. So the notion that either "I didn't have to do it for mine, for whatever reasons, and therefore have no intention of doing it for yours" or "Since I did it for mine I am not willing to do it for yours" is unreasonable and unfair.

An attitude of "Just because we did it for your mother doesn't mean we have to do it for your father" doesn't work. This is not a time to choose sides about who has a greater need. You have the same responsibility to your parents and to your wife's parents as she has to your parents and to her own parents. Difficult marriages, strained relationships, and midlife crises have a profound impact on your inability to respond to a parent's needs. These problems need to be acknowledged and understood.

If you are planing to provide care for your parents, or if you have provided care to yours, you should not be surprised to find your spouse assumes that you will now provide it for theirs. Again, clear communication early on will go a long way to avoid false expectations.

Often, the relationships with in-laws can be complicated, and feelings can run high when the question of their
care comes up. Again, if you have a good marriage, this
isn't a problem. But then, you may well have a good marriage except when it comes to this issue.

The struggle here is not so much what to do when, but
how to emotionally deal with the fallout from it, because
the more time that a parent requires from you as the caregiver, the less time you'll have available for others, especially your spouse. What if you come home from being
with mom for the day, having taken her to the doctor
or done some light cleaning in her apartment, and your
husband wants to know where dinner is? The emotional
strain for the spouse who is now feeling neglected may
be unreasonable but is, nonetheless, very real. Try to understand where the struggle really is. The issue may not be
that your husband expects dinner on the table when he gets
home. He may miss your companionship and he doesn't
know how to (or maybe can't) tell you.

Some of the issue here is finding a balance between
the emotional needs of your spouse with the physical-
care needs of your parent. The only limiting factor is
time. Think about how you can be as creative as possible
with the time you have, and be sure to "pencil in" some
time with your spouse. Again, call on your siblings and
other family members to help you if you are the primary
caregiver.

You have to also appreciate the bigger picture. As a
couple perhaps you have worked hard, struggled, raised

your children, sent the last one off to college, and forty-eight hours after you think, "Thank God, now it's time for me," your mother or your father-in-law needs care. Not only are you squeezed, your spouse is feeling squeezed as well.

Once again, communication is the key to dealing with this situation. Start by giving your spouse this book to read. Arrange a weekend away. If your siblings are unavailable, hire a companion, nurse, or a college student who is studying nursing, occupational therapy, physical therapy, social work, or a related field.

Some specific examples

Mary works in the public-relations department of a large company. Her husband, Ken, is a university professor who has just been offered a prestigious position as chairman of the history department of a college in a distant city. All of Mary and Ken's children are grown and working professionals.

Mary's mother, who has been diagnosed with Alzheimer's disease, has lived in her own apartment in a life-care setting. But now her illness requires her to live in a nursing home. Mary and Ken are suddenly confronted with a dilemma. His new position would require their moving one thousand miles away, but it's an opportunity that doesn't come along more than once or twice in a lifetime. Their choices are:

• He turns down the job so they can remain here, and then he's miserable.

- He takes the job, she goes with him and she sees her mother two or three times a year.

- They move and take mom with them to be placed in a facility.

- He takes the job, and she stays behind.

They chose the last option because they felt it would best answer everyone's needs, since the doctor's prognosis was that mom had only two or three years left to live. It hardly seemed fair to uproot her at this stage in her life, especially with the rest of her family, including grandchildren, close by. Mary and Ken also decided that although it would be difficult to live on her own, Mary could care for her mom more easily, and Ken could devote the time he needed for his new job. Though living apart would certainly put a strain on their relationship, it would serve mom best for a relatively short-term situation.

Another couple, Bill and Joan, faced a similar situation. She was offered a new job in California. Bill, a marketing consultant, operated his own business from their home in New York. Joan's mom, who had been living in senior housing, has mild dementia. The couple had been the primary caregivers for the last five years.

Though the medical concerns here were not as great as in the example above, the situation was more difficult with the prospect of commuting from New York to Los Angeles. They resolved the situation by moving mom to a nursing facility in Washington, D.C., where another sibling lived. The family met to discuss options, and decided that because Bill and Joan had taken care of mom and that now their lives were changing, it was time for someone else to take over.

There is almost always a solution when everybody is open, reasonable and willing to explore some options that may result in everyone being somewhat reasonably inconvenienced for the sake of the greater good of the family—including spouses. Sadly, there are times when compassion and understanding are in short supply. What happens when a spouse is intractable? Obviously there isn't any easy way out. However, don't forget there are professionals (psychiatrists, psychologists, social workers, etc.) available in every community to help you resolve any conflict. By all means use them if needed.

Chapter 10

Children

M any people look at their eldercare responsibilities as efforts they endure on their own as best they can. We think it is far more productive to view those around you as potential allies. Work to make those you live and work with part of the solution, not part of the problem. This includes your relationship with your children.

Children are, as we all know, naturally curious. Seeing their grandparents, regardless of their age or physical state, will prompt them to ask questions. As they look at you, they're bound to wonder, are you going to be like grandpa one day? Will they? Rather than perpetuate the idea that the glass is half empty, present it as being half full. Rather than approaching the issue as a negative, start a dialogue with your own kids about aging. Use this situation to help you in your task of caring for your parent.

Though it may be true that the decision to bring your parent into your home will be based on their needs, it is important not to overlook the benefits to your immediate family. This is especially true for the dual-career couple. Now you have, depending on your parent's health, a family member, who can be home and available in the afternoon when your children come home from school, at meal time to help with preparation, to provide child care and maybe even some light housecleaning. Sometimes what seemed like a burden you and your spouse were going to have to shoulder now becomes an agreeable situation.

If handled right, housing your parent under your roof can be a positive experience for children. They spend time with their grandparents, acquire an increased sense of family responsibility, and learn to appreciate firsthand the value you place on your parent.

The two main factors to consider are your child's (or children's) age and the degree of impairment and medical needs of your parent. Let's use the example we've used before: Grandma has fallen, broken her hip and requires treatment at the hospital. While the feeling is that she's recovering well and will eventually regain her former physical ability, she's going to require supervision for four to six weeks. This represents a limited length of stay for her at your house, and affords an opportunity to talk about obligations, responsibilities, love, and commitment with your children.

Sometimes, a family member may have to be inconvenienced for awhile. Grandma may have to move into Johnny's room. He'll have to double up with his little brother, which he's angry about. If part of the message you want your children to learn is how you would like to have them take care of you when the time comes, in essence, you're saying, "This is the way we handle these types of situations and care for one another in this family." If, on the other hand, you talk about and portray the situation as one in which your mother is coming in to intrude on the household but you have to put up with it because you feel guilty and you're stuck with it, that attitude will be transmitted to your children. You won't have succeeded in turning a negative situation into a positive opportunity to teach your children about responsibility.

What if mom is more mentally rather than physically impaired? Her speech and memory loss is confusing and at times very frightening to children, especially younger children. There are a host of very good, simple workbooks, such as Helping Grandma, published by Sandoz Pharmaceuticals, that are geared toward ten- to twelve-year-olds. Kids learn not to be frightened and that Grandma's behavior is not their fault but is a function of a medical condition she can't help.

Adolescents are often embarrassed by a grandparent's behavior. Try to make them understand the disease, as well as the fact that your family doesn't ignore a loved one who may be "impaired." The Alzheimer's Association runs support groups for spouses and children; check the Yellow Pages for locations.

Some people think that children shouldn't be exposed to people suffering mental impairment or be taken to nursing homes to visit an elderly relative. Our feeling is just the opposite. In fact, children are extremely therapeutic

for people living in long-term care settings, even if they are not able to recognize them. To deny your children an opportunity to participate in their grandparent's lives is to deny them a very rich and valuable experience.

Chapter 11

Work

The struggle of balancing the family, eldercare, and the workplace has become more difficult lately, with the rise of two-income households in America. During a crisis, most employers understand your need to be away from work to care for your parent. Once the acute problem is solved, however, many employers grow impatient with the regular distractions and demands that ongoing eldercare require. The more critical your role in the organization, the less understanding your superiors seem to be.

A story to illustrate

Let's look an example. Joanne, fifty-two, is married and works as an administrative assistant to the vice president of a multinational corporation. She is an only child; both her own children are grown and out of the house. She has spent nineteen years working her way up from a clerk-typist and has held her present position for the last five years. She supervises two secretaries, is responsible for her department's budget and financial projections, coordinates her boss's schedule, makes his travel plans, and plans conference agendas. She is truly her boss's right hand. He is appreciative of her efforts and has consistently made sure the company rewards her performance.

Joanne's seventy-five-year-old widowed mother has lived with her for seven years. While suffering from a number of chronic medical illnesses, including high blood pressure, insulin-dependent diabetes, and arthritis, she has been in generally good physical health. Over the last six months her eyesight has been failing, mostly as a result of her diabetes, and she was forced to surrender her driver's license. She has become increasingly dependent on Joanne. The once-daily check in phone call has been replaced with four or five calls each day. The regular quarterly visits to the doctor have given way to an increased number of aches and pains and hastily scheduled appointments with an array of specialists.

Joanne tried to balance work and home demands but the increased needs of her mother's care were clearly taking a toll. She was frequently leaving the office early or arriving late. She was often short tempered with her co-workers. Her work was often late or incomplete.

One Thursday morning, after returning from a three-day sales conference in Los Angeles, her boss called her into his office. When he asked her to shut the door and have a seat, she instantly knew he was angry. He wanted an explanation. His flight, car, and hotel reservations had gotten confused. Worse, material that was supposed to have been sent to California was not there when he arrived. When he called in Monday morning to speak with her, a secretary explained she was taking her mother to the doctor's and would, once again, be coming in late. Further, she'd never told the staff about sending the materials to the hotel.

Within thirty seconds Joanne was in tears, pouring out her heart to her boss. After listening patiently, he told her to immediately contact the company's EAP (Employee Assistance Program) coordinator. In many large companies, the EAP coordinator is responsible for helping employees with mental-health related problems, especially alcohol- and substance abuse-related issues. As dependent care of both children and parents has become a greater concern in the workplace, many companies have expanded the role of the EAP coordinator to also address these also.

To understand the importance of this development, one has to appreciate the reasons for lost productivity in corporate America. Substance abuse (both alcohol and drugs), accounts for some 30 percent of all lost work time. Dependant care ranks second, accounting for 24 percent of lost productivity. This not only includes time off from work to remain at home with ill children or parents, but also time taken to coordinate care, make trips to the doctor's office, and place multiple phone calls during the day. Some companies have done such an outstanding job of responding to their employees' dependent-care needs that they have received national recognition. Johnson & Johnson, IBM, Stride Rite, and Champion Corporation are a few. The Family and Medical Leave Act, passed by Congress in early

1993, mandates up to twelve weeks of unpaid leave for workers to care for a family member (whether a newborn or elderly relative).

Joanne met with one of the counselors and received a file full of information on local resources. Further, she learned that the company participated in a federal program that allowed pre-tax dollars to be deducted from Joanne's payroll for the use of her parent's care. The company also offered to pay for Joanne and her mom to be evaluated as well as a number of follow-up visits to stabilize the situation. The EAP coordinator also advised her to inform her co-workers about her situation. Rather than have to juggle all the stresses of work along with home and family herself, she could share some of her workload temporarily while she received outside assistance and put her eldercare responsibilities in order.

Soon Joanne hired a companion to be with mom and she returned to her normal work-performance level. She even resumed the social events she had put aside for so long.

Tips for handling the workplace

What can you do at work when you're feeling increasingly overwhelmed by your eldercare responsibilities?

• Inform your boss or supervisor about what's going on. Companies are concerned about the bottom line, but most realize the stress family crises can place on employee productivity and are willing, if not eager, to assist in resolving the situation. As in Joanne's case, you may be pleasantly surprised to find that your boss is actually a great source of information, assistance, and support.

• Talk to your coworkers. This has two potential benefits. First, it will allow them to better appreciate the stresses you're under and allow them to help alleviate some of your day-to-day burden. Second, it is very likely that one or more of your colleagues will have gone through a similar experience and be a valuable source of information.

• Contact your company's personnel, benefits, or human resources department. They will be able to put you in touch with your company's EAP coordinator or provide you with the company's policy for managing dependent-care issues.

• Ask your company how the Family and Medical Leave Act can work for you.

• Don't try and cover things up. Inevitably, the stress of trying to maintain a business-as-usual attitude will catch up with you. The sooner you acknowledge the situation, the sooner you can get assistance in resolving it.

• Explore work options your employer may offer or be willing to consider. Some allow for a flex-time schedule that allows you to maintain your full-time position (and pay) while manipulating your schedule around your care requirements. Though commonly used by parents coping with childcare issues, these options are increasingly used by those with eldercare responsibilities. Repeated studies have underscored that such unorthodox working arrangements can benefit the company as well as the employee.

Chapter 12

Yourself

The biggest misconception most adult children have about assuming the responsibility of caring for their aging parent is that somehow they're out there all alone.

In fact, the reality is that eldercare is the most rapidly growing section of the health care industry. Unless you're in a very isolated rural community, resources are available and only as far away as a phone call. Start to identify which resources you can use to help you manage. Chapter 3 identified some; Part Three lists national resources and explains how to find help in your or your parent's community. If you're willing to accept that caring for a parent can be an overwhelming task, even in the best of circumstances, and take advantage of these resources, you can decrease your own stress greatly. The greatest struggle facing geriatric psychiatry has not been with patients, but rather with their children, who have difficulty accepting diagnoses, realizing that mom or dad can't live alone anymore, stopping dad from driving the car, assuming responsibility for the finances, realizing that they, the children, can't do it all.

We all have limitations. Our capacity to cope with what life throws at us is very individual. There is no yard-stick by which we can measure how much we should be doing or how much responsibility we can carry. There is no doubt, however, that the more we try to manage alone, without accepting help, the more difficult the entire task becomes.

Studies show that fully one-third of all caregivers experience psychological symptoms—insomnia, anxiety, fatigue, easy distractibility, poor concentration, increased or diminished appetite, decreased libido, irritability, and often, when clustered together, depression—during the caregiving years. Often these caregivers are prescribed medication, but an unknown percentage take to alcohol or other nonprescription substances. It is not unusual for caregivers to begin to wish for the death of their parent, seeing this as a welcome relief from the burden of care-giving. This wish is especially evident in caregivers whose parents are affected with dementia. Realize that this wish does not make you a horrible person. It makes you human.

A specific example

Often caregivers fall into the trap of believing they must be the sole provider for their parents. Not only does this place the caregiver in an often impossible situation of try-ing to provide more (and more sophisticated) care than they are truly capable of, it causes tremendous emotional and physical stress. Sometimes the best thing to do is allow others, such as trained professionals, to help you identify and provide the assistance your parent needs. The following story illustrates this issue.

Sally, an accountant, moved her dad from New York two months prior to coming to our office for an evaluation. Dad was a seventy-four-year-old retired dentist, widowed for several years. He had closed his practice ten months earlier, at Sally's insistence, when she could no longer deny his symptoms of dementia, which made continued practice unsafe, both for his patients and for himself.

Sally arranged for a leave of absence from her job to care for her father, planning to return as soon as he was settled. Although she had left dad alone to run various errands with little difficulty, on several recent occasions she returned to potentially disastrous situations. Once dad had put a tea kettle on a stove burner and forgotten about it. Sally came home just in time to prevent a kitchen fire. On another occasion, dad had decided to take a walk and had gotten lost. When she returned home he was nowhere to be found. After ninety minutes of frantic searching throughout the neighborhood, she finally found him at a neighborhood convenience store where the police were questioning him, attempting to determine where he lived.

The evaluation was prompted by her employer, who was pressuring her either to return to work or resign. She needed and wanted to return to her job but realized that dad couldn't be left alone at all. She was convinced her only option was placing dad in a nursing home and simply could not accept "doing that to him," as she put it. After a ninety-minute evaluation we suggested:

- Adult day care three to five days per week, with home pickup at 8:30 a.m. and drop off at 3:30 p.m.

- A companion who would meet dad at the house at 3:30 p.m. and stay until Sally returned home from work at 5:30 p.m.

- A family conference with Sally, her brother who lived in Boston, and her sister who lived in Atlanta.

- An opportunity to meet with Sally's husband, who was initially very supportive of Sally's desire to care for her dad, but now, eight weeks later, was becoming increasingly annoyed with the entire arrangement.

- A conference between Sally and her boss to explore a flex-time schedule.

- Several books on Alzheimer's disease for her and her family's better understanding of the illness.

- An appreciation that with a little more time, support, and coordination, the entire situation could become manageable.

Sally took our suggestions. After visiting and evaluating several adult daycare centers, she enrolled her dad. She interviewed and hired a companion. Her brother and sister flew in for a family meeting. They agreed to not only contribute to dad's care costs but would come to Connecticut on a regular basis (or dad would go to Boston) to provide Sally with regular rest periods.

As dad became more comfortable with the companion, Sally and her husband were able to leave him in her care so they could enjoy a night out or even an occasional weekend away together. Sally was able to return to work ten days after the initial consultation, feeling somewhat guilty but relieved that dad was happy and being well cared for in her absence.

As dad's illness progressed over the next two years, however, it became increasingly difficult to leave him in the care of others. He was now having difficulty sleeping, episodes of incontinence, and increased confusion with paranoia. Sally was also feeling the increased stress, telling us that her marriage was in trouble and that she frequently fantasized about her father's dying and, of course, feeling horrible about even having such thoughts.

While we had occasionally talked about the possibility of nursing-home placement during the last two years (an option that Sally continued to reject), it was now clear that even with medication to control his behavior, the time had come to confront this issue. Another family conference, this one via telephone, followed. Both Sally's brother and sister were in full agreement with our suggestion of a nursing home. In fact, her brother and sister had actually researched nursing homes in both Boston and Atlanta without Sally's knowledge. They had made the decision that when the time came they would assume the responsibility for dad's nursing-home care and give Sally the break they both realized she needed to have. Finally, dad was admitted to a home in Atlanta, not far from the sister's house so she could now assume what had been Sally's job.

Three weeks later we saw Sally in our office. Much to her surprise, rather than feeling guilty about the nursing-home placement, she was tremendously relieved. She knew that her father was getting the quality care he needed. And her husband had expressed his sense of pride that she had been willing to do so much for her father. She was now at peace knowing she really had given it her all. Not surprisingly, she was sleeping better, working more productively, and really enjoying her marriage again.

Minimizing the toll of caregiving

Sally's story is not unique. Caring for anyone with a chronic, debilitating condition will take a toll on the caregiver. What can you do to mitigate the stresses and strains of caregiving? The first step is to realize just how difficult the endeavor may prove to be. In doing that, you will realize you must look to others. Begin to establish boundaries for yourself.

Chapter 3 explains how to know when you need help. Say to yourself, I'll need a companion when x happens, I'll need a day off when y occurs, I'll need a vacation at such and such a time, and so on. If your parent lives with you, you may find that quiet time at home is diminished. We encourage caregivers to take respite breaks at home. Arrange for a sibling or adult child to take your parent for a day or weekend. The sense of rejuvenation can be remarkable.

More tips for caregivers

Seek support: Many national self-help groups have local chapters that run monthly support groups for caregivers. Part Three contains a listing. Perhaps the best known is the Alzheimer's Association based in Chicago. Founded in 1980, it boasts chapters in every state and maintains more than eleven thousand support groups nationwide. Contact them. Find out where and when these groups meet. They provide you with the chance to learn more about the illness, the latest research, names of good doctors in your community, additional community resources, the opportunity to talk with others who are going through a similar experience, and, perhaps most important, the chance to make new friends who understand and appreciate what you're dealing with as a caregiver.

Seek professional help for yourself: In our clinical practice during the last ten years, we have seen and worked with approximately four thousand patients and their families, from laborers to university deans, from secretaries to corporate CEOs. Almost 25 percent of the time, we have suggested caregivers seek help for themselves separate from the help they are seeking for their parent.

Perhaps half did; they were able to remain in the role of active caregiver longer and feel a greater sense of satisfaction then those who did not. They were also better able to accept nursing-home placement or other difficult decisions with less guilt.

Use relaxation techniques: A February 1992 article

in *Consumer Reports* addressed the use of medication in treatment for anxiety disorders. While the article was generally opposed to the use of anti-anxiety medication, it did point out the positive aspects of therapeutic intervention, behavioral techniques that one can learn to control anxiety. Receiving instruction for biofeedback, listening to relaxation tapes, or taking a seminar on stress management can be helpful.

Don't say, "I don't have the time or energy to take a class, or listen to tapes; just give me a pill." The goal here is for you to regain a sense of control over your situation, rather than having the situation completely dominate you. There may be a time and place for medication, but try all the suggestions in this book first.

An ounce of prevention is worth a pound of cure: Often the question of when to intervene with a parent's affairs is as crucial as the caregiving that may follow. This situation is exemplified by Diane, forty-seven, a married insurance executive. During a semi-annual trip to Florida to visit her parents, Diane was struck by her mom's inability to perform her customary household chores. She was clearly having difficulty cooking, cleaning, and generally keeping house. Perhaps even more surprising was that her father, the guy whose daily routine was to return home from work, read the paper while mom prepared dinner, eat, then return to his chair for a night in front of the television, had assumed all of mom's physical and social duties. She didn't think dad knew where the washing machine was, much less how to use it.

As nice as it was to see dad pitching in, Diane couldn't deny the truth of what she was seeing. When she confronted her father about mom, he minimized her difficulties. He said she was simply "getting older." Though Diane pressed the point and strongly suggested they take mom to a doctor to be evaluated, he refused.

Diane returned home. Back at work, she called her company's EAP (Employee Assistance Program) coordinator and was referred to our office for assistance. A brief telephone conversation highlighted the issues and a one-hour, in-office consultation clarified her concerns. "How can I help my parents when I'm fifteen hundred miles away? I go to bed every night afraid the phone will ring with horrible news. I call my dad every day just to make sure everything's okay. But I can't be sure he's telling me the truth. I feel so helpless."

As we got a better understanding of the situation from Diane and a better appreciation of her relationship to her parents, it became easier to map out a strategy. While mom's memory loss indicated an evaluation was clearly needed, not all memory loss is a sign of dementia, and without other symptoms it wasn't viewed as critical. In truth, there was really nothing that Diane needed to do for her mother at this moment. Far more pressing was Diane's perception that she needed to do something immediately.

The "something" we assigned her was to begin to identify appropriate resources near her parents in Florida. We referred her to the local offices of Jewish Family Services and Catholic Family Services, both of which could give her the appropriate contact numbers in Florida. We suggested she contact the Florida Department of Aging, and gave her the numbers for a geriatric psychiatrist and internist who practiced near her parents. This information helped relieve her anxiety as she now knew who to call if and when the crises she feared actually materialized.

Two months later Diane called again to tell us that her parents were coming north for a visit and she wanted to set up an appointment to have mom evaluated. Though her father still maintained this was a waste of time and money, he finally agreed. What changed his mind? In Florida, he viewed Diane as an intruder who had no right to come into his home and decide how he and mom should live their lives. But after Diane presented the examination as her way to feel better about the situation, he reluctantly acquiesced to her position as concerned daughter. The examination showed mom was suffering more from depression than dementia. Dad agreed to extend their stay for an additional month so we could evaluate the impact of an antidepressant medication. They eventually returned to Florida. Mom was seen by one of our colleagues in Miami for a follow up to treatment.

Was Diane's effort wasted? Absolutely not. If mom had been diagnosed with Alzheimer's disease and not depression, Diane, who had already done her homework, would have been poised to intervene with the appropriate local care providers. Thankfully it wasn't necessary. But Diane's story points up the ease of obtaining information. Diane didn't have to leave her office to have an entire contingency plan at her disposal. She took appropriate action at the appropriate time and was able to feel good knowing she'd played an active role in her mother's care.

Finally, some things to do for yourself

• Schedule a night out and arrange for others (a spouse, your children, a trusted neighbor, a paid companion) to be with your parent.

• Enroll in an adult-education course to give yourself something to look forward to each week.

• Plan vacation time so you can get away for a few days every few weeks or months while someone else cares for your parent in your home.

• Arrange for a change of scene for your parent, so you can have a couple of days or a week every few months to yourself in your home.

• Don't be a hero. There's nothing wrong with acknowledging that you have a tough job to do. You don't have to do it alone, and it's much better if you acknowledge your limitations and willingly accept help. Such an attitude will help you stay in the role of caregiver as long as it is neccessary and appropriate to do so.

Part III

Resources & References

Resources

Alzheimer's Association
919 North Michigan
Chicago, IL 60611
(312) 335-8700

Founded in 1980, this private, nonprofit organization provides education, community-based support, research funding and advocacy for people afflicted with Alzheimer's Disease and their families.

American Geriatrics Society
770 Lexington Avenue, Suite 400
New York, NY 10021
(212) 308-1414

Approximately 5,400 health-care professionals, primarily physicians from around the world, who are devoted to the clinical care of the elderly.

American Health Care Association
1200 Fifteenth Street, N.W.
Washington, D.C. 20005
(202) 833-2050

Nonprofit federation of associations from each of the
fifty states plus Washington, D.C., serving 950,000
residents of nearly 9,500 licensed nursing homes and
allied facilities.

American Psychiatric Association
1400 K Street, N.W.
Washington, D.C . 20005
(202) 682-6000

Professional society of approximately 36,000 psychiatrists
throughout the United States.

American Psychological Association
1200 Seventeenth Street, N.W.
Washington, D.C. 20036
(202) 955-7600

Professional society of more than 65,000 psychologists
throughout the United States.

American Society for Geriatric Dentistry
211 East Chicago Avenue
Chicago, IL 60611
(312) 353-6547, (312) 664-8270

A medical society comprised of dentists who specialize in
treatment of the elderly.

American Society on Aging
833 Market Street, Suite 512
San Francisco, CA 94103
(415) 543-2617

A national nonprofit membership organization of
practitioners, educators, researchers, and others in the
field of aging.

Association for Gerontology
in Higher Education
600 Maryland Avenue, S. W.
West Wing 204
Washington, D.C. 20024
(202) 484-7505

Membership of more than 200 colleges and universities
whose purpose is to foster the development and increase
the commitment of higher education in the field of aging
through education, research, and public service.

Children of Aging Parents
2761 Trenton Road
Levittown, PA 19056
(215) 547-1070

CAPS is an organization of adult children involved
in parentcare that will help you find support groups in
your area.

Gerontological Society of America
1411 K Street, N.W., Suite 300
Washington, D.C. 20005
(202) 393-1411

A 6,500-member, multidisciplinary professional organization devoted to bettering the condition of the aged through research and education.

Gray Panthers
311 South Juniper Street, Suite 601
Philadelphia, PA 19107
(215) 545-6555

National group with 75,000 or more members in more than 100 chapters focused on activities aimed to improve health, social, economic, and political conditions in the United States, especially for older Americans.

Huntington Disease Society of America, Inc.
140 West Twenty-second Street
New York, NY 10011-2420
(212) 242-1968

National Association for Home Care
519 C Street, N.E., Stanton Park
Washington, D.C. 20002
(202) 547-7424

NAHC is a national clearinghouse of information on home-care agencies.

National Association for Spanish Speaking Elderly
2025 I Street, N.W., Suite 219
Washington, DC 20006
(202) 293-9329

National Association of Meal Programs
204 E Street, N.E.
Washington, DC 20006
(202) 547-6157

More than 800 individual, organization, and corporate
members who deliver meals to older persons at home and
in group settings. Most provide technical assistance,
information exchange, and leadership for legislation.

National Association of Social Workers
7981 Eastern Avenue
Silver Spring, MD 20910
(301) 565-0333

Professional society of approximately 109,000 social
workers throughout the United States.

National Council on the Aging, Inc.
600 Maryland Avenue, S.W.
West Wing 100
Washington, D.C. 20024
(202) 479-1200

A representative organization responsible for the
distribution of information, educational opportunities,
and research funding as it relates to aging.

National Institutes of Health
9000 Rockville Pike
Bethesda, MD 20814
(310) 496-1752

America's national health related research organization.

National Institute of Mental Health
Mental Disorders of the Aging Research Branch, DCR
Room 11C-03
5600 Fishers Lane
Rockville, MD 20857
(301) 443-1185

The institute within the NIH dedicated exclusively to mental health related issues.

Veterans Administration
810 Vermont Avenue, N.W.
Washington, DC 20420
(202) 233-4000

Provides health care for all of America's armed services veterans.

LIVING WILL

I,   , of the Town of   , County of   and State of   , being of sound mind, willfully and voluntarily make known my desire that my dying shall not be artificially prolonged under the circumstances set forth below, do hereby declare:

If at any time I should have an incurable injury, disease, or illness regarded as a terminal condition by my physician and if my physician has determined that the application of life-sustaining procedures would serve only to artificially prolong the dying process and that my death will occur whether or not life-sustaining procedures are utilized, I direct that such procedures be withheld or withdrawn and that I be permitted to die with only the merciful administration of medication to eliminate or reduce pain to my mind or body or the performance of any medical procedure deemed necessary to provide me with comfort care.

In the absence of my ability to give directions regarding the use of such life-sustaining procedures, it is my intention that this declaration shall be honored by my family and physician as the final expression of my legal right to refuse medical or surgical treatment and accept the consequences from such refusal.

I understand the full import of this declaration and I am emotionally and mentally competent to make this declaration.

DATED this   day of   , 19   .

_____

The declarant has been personally known to me and I believe her/him to be of sound mind.

_____ Witness

_____ Witness

State Agencies
on the Aging

Alabama
Commission on Aging
State Capitol
Montgomery, AL 36130
(205) 261-5743

Alaska
Older Alaskans Commision
Dept. of Administration
Pouch C-Mail Station 0209
Juneau, AK 99811
(907) 465-3250

Arizona
Aging and Adult Administration
Dept. of Economic Security
1400 W. Washington St.
Phoenix, AZ 85007
(602) 255-4446

Arkansas
Office of Aging & Adult Services
Dept. of Social & Rehabilitation Services
Donaghey Bldg. Suite 1428
7th & Main Streets
Little Rock, AR 72201

California
Dept. of Aging
1020 19th St.
Sacramento, CA 95814
(916) 322-5290

Colorado
Aging & Adult Services Div.
Dept. of Social Services
1575 Sherman St. Room 503
Denver, CO 80203
(303) 866-3672

Connecticut
Dept. of Aging
175 Main St.
Hartford, CT 06106
(203) 566-3238

Delaware
Div. on Aging
Dept. of Health & Social Services
1901 N. DuPont Hwy.
Newcastle, DE 19720
(302) 421-6791

District of Columbia
Office on Aging
1424 K St. NW, 2nd Floor
Washington, D.C. 20011
(202) 724-5626

Florida
Program Office of Aging & Adult
   Services
Dept. of Health & Rehabilitation Services
1317 Winewood Blvd.
Tallahassee, FL 32301
(904) 488-8922

Georgia
Office of Aging
878 Peachtree St. NE, Room 632
Atlanta, GA 30309
(404) 894-5333

Guam
Public Health & Social Services
Government of Guam
Agana, GU 96910

Hawaii
Executive Office on Aging
Office of the Governor
1149 Bethel St., Room 307
Honolulu, HI 96813
(808) 548-2593

Idaho
Office on Aging
Statehouse, Room 114
Boise, ID 83720
(208) 334-3833

Indiana
Dept. of Aging & Community Services
Consolidated Bldg. Suite 1350
115 N. Pennsylvania St.
Indianapolis, IN 46204

Iowa
Iowa Dept. of Elder Affairs
Jewett Bldg. Suite 236
914 Grand Ave.
Des Moines, IA 50319
(515) 281-5187

Kansas
Dept. on Aging
610 W. 10th St.
Topeka, KS 66612
(913) 296-4986

Kentucky
Div. for Aging Services
Dept. of Human Resources
DHR Bldg. 6th Floor
275 E. Main St.
Frankfort, KY 40601
(502) 564-6930

Louisiana
Office of Elderly Affairs
P.O. Box 83074
Baton Rouge, LA 70898
(504) 925-1700

Maine
Bureau of Maine's Elderly
Dept. of Human Services
State House, Station #11
Augusta, ME 04333
(207) 289-2561

Mariana Islands
Office of Elderly Programs
Community Development Div.
Government of TTPI
Saipan, Mariana Islands 96950
Tel: 9335 or 9336

Maryland
Office on Aging
State Office Bldg. Room 1004
301 W. Preston St.
Baltimore, MD 21201
(301) 383-5064

Massachusetts
Dept. of Elder Affairs
38 Chauncy St.
Boston, MA 02111
(617) 727-7750

Michigan
Office of Services to the Aging
P.O. Box 30026
Lansing, MI 48909
(517) 373-8230

Minnesota
Board on Aging
Metro Square Bldg. Room 204
7th & Robert Streets
St. Paul, MN 55101
(612) 296-2544

Mississippi
Council on Aging
Executive Bldg. Suite 301
802 N. State St.
Jackson, MS 39201
(601) 354-6590

Missouri
Div. on Aging
Dept. of Social Services
Broadway State Office
P.O. Box 570
Jefferson City, MO 65101
(314) 751-3082

Montana
Community Services Bureau
P.O. Box 4210
Helena, MT 39604
(406) 444-3865

Nevada
Div. on Aging
Dept. of Human Resources
Kinkead Bldg. Room 101
505 E. King St.
Carson City, NV 89710
(702) 885-4210

New Hampshire
Council on Aging
14 Depot St.
Concord, NH 03301
(603) 271-2751

New Jersey
Div. on Aging
Dept. of Community Affairs
363 W. State St.
Trenton, NJ 08625
(609) 292-4833

New Mexico
State Agency on Aging
La Villa Rivera Bldg. 4th Floor
224 E. Palace Ave.
Santa Fe, NM 85601
(505) 827-7640

New York
Office for the Aging
New York State Plaza, Agency Bldg. 2
Albany, NY 12223
(518) 474-4425

North Carolina
Div. on Aging
708 Hillsborough St., Suite 200
Raleigh, NC 27603
(919) 733-3983

North Dakota
Aging Services
Dept. of Human Services
State Capitol Building
Bismark, ND 58505
(701) 224-2577

Northern Mariana Islands
Office of Aging
Dept. of Comm. & Cultural Affairs
Civic Center
Susupe, Saipan, N. Mariana Islands 96950
Tel: 9411 or 9732

Ohio
Dept. on Aging
50 West Broad St., 9th Floor
Columbus, OH 43215
(614) 466-5500

Oklahoma
Special Unit on Aging
Dept. of Human Services
P.O. Box 25352
Oklahoma City, OK 73125
(405) 521-2281

Oregon
Senior Services Div.
313 Public Service Bldg
Salem, OR 97310
(503) 378-4728

Pennsylvania
Dept. on Aging
231 State St.
Harrisburg, PA 17101-1195
(717) 783-1550

Puerto Rico
Gericulture Commission
Dept. of Social Services
P.O. Box 11398
Santurce, PR 00910
(809) 724-7400 or
(809) 725-8015

Rhode Island
Dept. of Elderly Affairs
79 Washington St.
Povidence, RI 02903
(401) 277-2858

(American) Samoa
Territorial Administration on Aging
Office of the Governor
Pago Pago, AS 96799
011-6848-633-1252

South Carolina
Commission of Aging
915 Main St.
Columbia, SC 29201
(803) 758-2576

South Dakota
Office of Adult Services & Aging
Kneip Bldg.
700 N. Illinois St.
Pierre, SD 57501
(605) 773-3656

Tennessee
Commission on Aging
715 Tennessee Bldg.
Nashville, TN 37219
(615) 741-2056

Texas
Dept. on Aging
210 Barton Springs Rd. 5th Floor
P.O. Box 12768 Capitol Station
Austin, TX 78704
(512) 475-2712

Utah
Div. of Aging & Adult Services
Dept. of Social Services
150 West North Temple
Box 2500
Salt Lake City, UT 84102
(801) 533-6422

Vermont
Office on Aging
103 S. Main St.
Waterbury, VT 05676
(802) 241-2400

Virgin Islands
Commission on Aging
6F Havensight Mall
Charlotte Amalie, St. Thomas, VI 00801
(809) 774-5884

Washington
Bureau of Aging & Adult Services
Dept. of Social & Health Services
OB-34G
Olympia, WA 98504
(206) 753-2502

West Virginia
Commission on Aging
Holly Grove-State Capitol
Charleston, WV 25305
(304) 348-3317

Wisconsin
Bureau of Aging
Div. of Community Services
One W. Wilson St., Room 663
P.O. Box 7850
Madison, WI 53702
(608) 266-2536

Wyoming
Commission on Aging
Hathaway Bldg. Room 139
Cheyenne, WY 82002-0710
(307) 777-7986

Table 1— Expectation of Life (in Years)
United States, 1979-81 to 1992

| Age | National Center for Health Statistics | | | | Metropolitan Life Insurance Company |
	1979-81	1989	1990	1991*	1992*
Total Population					
0	73.9	75.3	75.4	75.5	75.7
15	60.2	61.3	61.3	61.5	61.6
25	50.8	51.9	51.9	52.1	52.2
35	41.4	42.5	42.6	42.7	42.8
45	32.3	33.4	33.4	33.6	33.7
55	23.9	24.7	24.8	24.9	25.0
65	16.5	17.2	17.2	17.4	17.5
75	10.5	10.9	10.9	11.1	11.1
05	6.0	6.2	6.1	6.2	6.3
Male					
0	70.1	71.8	71.8	72.0	72.2
15	56.5	57.9	57.9	58.0	58.2
25	47.4	48.7	48.7	48.8	48.9
35	38.2	39.6	39.6	39.7	39.8
45	29.2	30.7	30.7	30.8	31.0
55	21.1	22.3	22.3	22.4	22.5
65	14.2	15.2	15.1	15.2	15.3
75	8.9	9.4	9.4	9.5	9.5
85	5.1	5.3	5.2	5.3	5.3
Female					
0	77.6	78.6	78.8	79.0	79.1
15	63.8	64.6	64.7	64.9	64.9
25	54.2	54.9	55.0	55.2	55.2
35	44.5	45.3	45.3	45.5	45.6
45	35.2	35.8	35.9	36.1	36.2
55	26.4	26.9	27.0	27.1	27.2
65	18.4	18.8	18.9	19.1	19.1
75	11.6	11.9	12.0	12.1	12.2
85	6.4	6.6	6.4	6.6	6.7

*Estimated.

149

Table 2 — Expectation of Life at Selected Ages, by Race and Sex, United States, 1900-02 to 1991

| | Expectation of Life (in Years) | | | | | |
| | | | White | | | |
Age	1900-02	1949-51	1979-81	1989	1990	1991*
Male						
0	48.2	66.3	70.8	72.7	72.7	73.0
15	46.3	54.2	57.1	58.6	58.6	58.9
25	38.5	44.9	47.9	49.4	49.3	49.7
35	31.3	35.7	38.7	40.1	40.1	40.4
45	24.2	26.9	29.6	31.1	31.1	31.4
55	17.4	19.1	21.3	22.5	22.5	22.9
65	11.5	12.8	14.3	15.2	15.2	15.5
75	6.8	7.8	8.9	9.4	9.4	9.5
85	3.8	4.4	5.1	5.3		5.4
Female						
0	51.1	72.0	78.2	79.2	79.4	79.7
15	47.8	59.4	64.3	65.1	65.2	65.4
25	40.1	49.8	54.6	55.3	55.4	55.7
35	32.8	40.3	44.9	45.7	45.8	46.0
45	25.5	31.1	35.5	36.1	36.2	36.5
55	18.4	22.6	26.6	27.1	27.2	27.4
65	12.2	15.0	18.6	19.0	19.1	19.3
75	7.3	8.9	11.6	11.9	12.0	12.2
85	4.1	4.8	6.3	6.5	6.4	6.8

* Provisional

	Expectation of Life (in Years)										
	All Other Total					Black					
Age	1949 -51*	1979 -81	1989	1990	1991*	1900 -1902	1949 -51	1979 -81	1989	1990	1991*
Male											
0	58.9	65.6	67.1	67.0	68.1	32.5		64.1	64.8	64.5	65.6
15	48.2	52.5	53.8	53.6	54.5	38.3		51.1	51.6	51.3	52.3
25	39.5	43.5	44.8	44.6	45.7	32.2		42.1	42.7	42.4	43.6
35	31.2	34.8	36.2	36.0	37.2	26.2		33.6	34.3	34.1	35.2
45	23.6	26.6	28.2	27.8	29.1	20.1	N/A	25.6	26.6	26.2	27.4
55	17.4	19.6	20.8	20.3	21.5	14.7		18.8	19.0	19.0	20.0
65	12.8	13.8	14.5	14.0	15.2	10.4		13.3	13.6	13.2	14.2
75	8.8	9.2	9.4	9.1	10.1	6.6		8.9	8.8	8.6	9.3
85	5.4	5.7	5.8	5.3	6.4	4.0		5.6	5.6	5.0	6.0
Female											
0	62.7	74.0	75.2	75.2	76.2	35.0		72.9	73.5	73.6	74.3
15	51.4	60.7	61.7	61.7	62.6	39.8		59.7	60.2	60.2	60.9
25	42.4	51.1	52.1	52.0	53.0	33.9		50.1	50.6	50.6	51.3
35	33.8	41.7	42.7	42.6	43.5	27.5		40.8	41.3	41.3	42.0
45	26.1	32.8	33.7	33.6	34.5	21.4	N/A	31.9	32.4	32.4	33.1
55	19.6	24.7	25.3	25.1	26.0	15.9		24.0	24.1	24.2	24.8
65	14.5	17.6	17.9	17.8	18.6	11.4		17.1	17.0	17.2	17.5
75	10.2	11.7	11.6	11.5	12.3	7.9		11.4	11.0	11.2	11.5
85	6.2	7.2	6.9	6.4	7.4	5.1		7.1	6.7	6.3	7.0

* 1900 — 02 N/A   Source: Various reports by the National Center for Health Statistics.

Table 3 A—Expectation of Life Rates
at Single Years of Age by Race and Sex

	Expectation of Life (in Years)				
	Total	White		All Other	
Age	Persons	Male	Female	Male	Female
0	75.4	72.7	79.4	67.0	75.2
1	75.1	72.3	78.9	67.2	75.3
2	74.1	71.4	78.0	66.2	74.4
3	73.1	70.4	77.0	65.3	73.4
4	72.2	69.4	76.0	64.3	72.5
5	71.2	68.5	75.0	63.4	71.6
6	70.2	67.5	74.1	62.4	70.5
7	69.2	66.5	73.1	61.4	69.5
8	68.2	65.5	72.1	60.4	68.5
9	67.3	64.5	71.1	59.4	67.6
10	66.3	63.5	70.1	58.5	66.6
11	65.3	62.6	69.1	57.5	65.6
12	64.3	61.6	68.1	56.5	64.6
13	63.3	60.6	67.1	55.5	63.6
14	62.3	59.6	66.2	54.5	62.6
15	61.3	58.6	65.2	53.6	61.7
16	60.4	57.7	64.2	52.6	60.7
17	59.4	56.7	63.2	51.7	59.7
18	58.5	55.8	62.3	50.8	58.7
19	57.5	54.9	61.3	49.9	57.8
20	56.6	54.0	60.3	49.0	56.8
21	55.7	53.0	59.3	48.1	55.8
22	54.7	52.1	58.4	47.3	54.9
23	53.8	51.2	57.4	46.4	53.9
24	52.8	50.3	56.4	45.5	53.0
25	51.9	49.3	55.4	44.6	52.0
26	51.0	48.4	54.5	43.8	51.0
27	50.0	47.5	53.5	42.9	50.1
28	49.1	46.6	52.5	42.0	49.2
29	48.1	45.6	51.6	41.2	48.2
30	47.2	44.7	50.6	40.3	47.3
31	46.3	43.8	49.6	39.4	46.3
32	45.3	42.9	48.7	38.6	45.4
33	44.4	41.9	47.7	37.7	44.5
34	43.5	41.0	46.7	36.9	43.5
35	42.6	40.1	45.8	36.0	42.6
36	41.6	39.2	44.8	35.2	41.7
37	40.7	38.3	43.8	34.4	40.8
38	39.8	37.4	42.9	33.5	39.9
39	38.9	36.5	41.9	32.7	39.0

Vital Statistics of the United States, 1990;

Vol. II Sec 6, Life Tables, DHHS Publication No. (PHS 93-1104)

Table 3 A — Expectation of Life Rates at Single Years of Age by Race and Sex cont.

		Expectation of Life (in Years)			
	Total	White		All Other	
Age	Persons	Male	Female	Male	Female
40	38.0	35.6	41.0	31.9	38.1
41	37.0	34.7	40.0	31.1	37.1
42	36.1	33.8	39.1	30.3	36.2
43	35.2	32.9	38.1	29.4	35.5
44	34.3	32.0	37.2	28.6	34.4
45	33.4	31.1	36.2	27.8	33.6
46	32.5	30.2	35.3	27.0	32.7
47	31.6	29.3	34.4	26.3	31.8
48	30.7	28.4	33.5	25.5	30.9
49	29.9	27.6	32.5	24.7	30.1
50	29.0	26.7	31.6	23.9	29.2
51	28.1	25.8	30.7	23.2	28.4
52	27.3	25.0	29.8	22.4	27.6
53	26.4	24.2	29.0	21.7	26.7
54	25.6	23.3	28.1	21.0	25.9
55	24.8	22.5	27.2	20.3	25.1
56	24.0	21.7	26.4	19.6	24.3
57	23.2	21.0	25.5	18.9	23.6
58	22.4	20.2	24.7	18.3	22.8
59	21.6	19.4	23.8	17.6	22.0
60	20.8	18.7	23.0	17.0	21.3
61	20.1	18.0	22.2	16.4	20.6
62	19.4	17.3	21.4	15.8	19.9
63	18.6	16.6	20.6	15.2	19.1
64	17.9	15.9	19.8	14.6	18.5
65	17.2	15.2	19.1	14.0	17.8
66	16.5	14.6	18.3	13.5	17.1
67	15.9	13.9	17.5	12.9	16.4
68	15.2	13.3	16.8	12.4	15.8
69	14.5	12.7	16.1	11.9	15.2
70	13.9	12.1	15.4	11.4	14.5
71	13.3	11.5	14.7	10.9	13.9
72	12.7	11.0	14.0	10.5	13.3
73	12.1	10.4	13.3	10.0	12.7
74	11.5	9.9	12.6	9.5	12.1
75	10.9	9.4	12.0	9.1	11.5
76	10.4	8.9	11.4	8.7	10.9
77	9.8	8.4	10.8	8.3	10.4
78	9.3	7.9	10.2	7.8	9.8
79	8.8	7.5	9.6	7.4	9.3
80	8.3	7.1	9.0	7.0	8.8
81	7.8	6.7	8.4	6.7	8.2
82	7.4	6.3	7.9	6.3	7.7
83	6.9	5.9	7.4	5.9	7.3
84	6.5	5.5	6.9	5.6	6.8
85	6.1	5.2	6.4	5.3	6.4

Table 3 B — Expectation of Mortality Rates at Single Years of Age by Race and Sex

| | Mortality Rate per 1,000 | | | | |
| | Total | White | | All Other | |
Age	Persons	Male	Female	Male	Female
0	9.3	8.6	6.6	17.0	14.1
1	0.7	0.7	0.5	1.1	0.8
2	0.5	0.5	0.4	0.8	0.6
3	0.4	0.4	0.3	0.6	0.5
4	0.3	0.3	0.3	0.5	0.4
5	0.3	0.3	0.2	0.4	0.3
6	0.3	0.3	0.2	0.4	0.3
7	0.2	0.3	0.2	0.4	0.2
8	0.2	0.2	0.2	0.3	0.2
9	0.2	0.2	0.1	0.2	0.2
10	0.2	0.2	0.1	0.2	0.2
11	0.2	0.2	0.1	0.2	0.2
12	0.2	0.2	0.2	0.3	0.2
13	0.3	0.4	0.2	0.5	0.3
14	0.5	0.6	0.3	0.8	0.3
15	0.6	0.8	0.4	1.2	0.4
16	0.8	1.0	0.4	1.5	0.5
17	0.9	1.2	0.5	1.8	0.5
18	1.0	1.3	0.5	2.1	0.6
19	1.0	1.4	0.5	2.2	0.6
20	1.0	1.4	0.5	2.4	0.6
21	1.1	1.4	0.5	2.5	0.7
22	1.1	1.5	0.5	2.6	0.7
23	1.1	1.5	0.5	2.7	0.8
24	1.2	1.5	0.5	2.8	0.9
25	1.2	1.5	0.5	2.9	0.9
26	1.2	1.6	0.5	3.0	1.0
27	1.2	1.6	0.5	3.1	1.1
28	1.3	1.6	0.6	3.2	1.2
29	1.3	1.7	0.6	3.4	1.3
30	1.4	1.8	0.6	3.5	1.4
31	1.5	1.8	0.7	3.7	1.5
32	1.5	1.9	0.7	3.9	1.6
33	1.6	2.0	0.7	4.1	1.7
34	1.7	2.1	0.8	4.4	1.8
35	1.8	2.2	0.8	4.6	1.9
36	1.9	2.3	0.9	4.9	2.0
37	2.0	2.4	1.0	5.1	2.1
38	2.1	2.5	1.0	5.3	2.2
39	2.2	2.6	1.1	5.5	2.3

Vital Statistics of the United States, 1990;

Vol. II Sec 6, Life Tables, DHHS Publication No. (PHS 93-1104)

Table 3 B — Expectation of Mortality Rates at Single Years of Age by Race and Sex cont.

	Mortality Rate per 1,000				
	Total	White		All Other	
Age	Persons	Male	Female	Male	Female
40	2.2	2.7	1.2	5.7	2.5
41	2.4	2.8	1.3	5.9	2.6
42	2.5	3.0	1.4	6.2	2.8
43	2.7	3.2	1.6	6.5	3.0
44	2.9	3.4	1.7	7.0	3.3
45	3.2	3.7	1.9	7.5	3.6
46	3.4	4.0	2.1	8.0	3.9
47	3.7	4.3	2.4	8.5	4.3
48	4.1	4.7	2.6	9.1	4.7
49	4.4	5.1	2.9	9.7	5.1
50	4.9	5.6	3.2	10.4	5.6
51	5.3	6.1	3.5	11.1	6.0
52	5.8	6.8	3.9	12.0	6.6
53	6.4	7.5	4.3	13.0	7.2
54	7.0	8.3	4.7	14.2	7.8
55	7.7	9.1	5.2	15.4	8.5
56	8.4	10.0	5.7	16.8	9.2
57	9.2	11.1	6.2	18.2	10.0
58	10.1	12.2	6.9	19.6	10.9
59	11.1	13.5	7.6	21.1	11.8
60	12.2	15.0	8.4	22.8	12.8
61	13.3	16.5	9.2	24.5	13.9
62	14.5	18.0	10.0	26.2	15.0
63	15.7	19.6	10.9	28.1	16.1
64	16.9	21.2	11.8	30.0	17.4
65	18.2	23.0	12.8	32.0	18.7
66	19.7	24.9	13.8	34.1	20.2
67	21.3	27.0	15.1	36.5	21.6
68	23.1	29.4	16.5	39.1	23.1
69	25.1	32.2	18.1	41.9	24.7
70	27.3	35.2	19.8	45.0	26.4
71	29.7	38.3	21.7	48.3	28.2
72	32.2	41.7	23.7	51.6	30.1
73	34.9	45.5	25.9	55.0	32.3
74	37.9	49.5	28.4	58.4	34.6
75	41.1	53.9	31.1	62.0	37.2
76	44.6	58.6	34.1	65.9	40.0
77	48.4	63.8	37.4	70.2	43.1
78	52.5	69.3	41.1	75.0	46.6
79	57.1	75.4	45.2	80.3	50.6
80	62.2	82.0	49.9	86.2	55.1
81	67.9	89.3	55.3	92.7	60.3
82	74.4	97.2	61.4	99.7	66.3
83	81.6	106.0	68.6	107.3	73.4
84	90.0	115.7	77.0	115.2	81.8
85					

Suggested Reading
for the Adult Caregiver

Aronson, Miriam K., Ed., *Understanding Alzheimer's Disease: What It Is, How to Cope With It, Future Directions* Alzheimer's Disease & Related Disorders Association. New York: Charles Scribner's Sons, 1988. ★

Dychtwald, Ken, Ph. D., *Age Wave: The Challenges and Opportunities of an Aging America* Los Angeles: Jeremy P. Tarcher, Inc. Distributed by St. Martin's Press, New York, 1989.

Edinberg, Mark A., *Talking with Your Aging Parents: An Expert in Counseling the Elderly and Their Families Offers Strategies, Skills, and Support for Communications with Older Relatives About Difficult Issues Like Failing Health, Legal and Financial Matters, and Family Relations* Boston: Shambala Publications, Inc. Distributed by Random House, 1987.

Jarvick, Lissy, M.D., Ph.D. and Small, Gary, M.D., *Parentcare: A Commonsense Guide for Adult Children* New York: Crown Publishers, Inc. 1988.

Mace, Nancy L. and Robins, Peter V., M.D.. *The 36-Hour Day: A Family Guide to Caring for Persons with Alzheimer's Disease, Related Dementing Illness, and Memory Loss in Later Life* Baltimore: The Johns Hopkins University Press, 1981.★

Shelley, Florence D., *When Your Parents Grow Old: Information and Resources to Help the Adult Son or Daughter Cope with the Problems of Aging Parents* New York: Harper & Row, Publishers, 1988.

Wharton, William, *DAD* New York: Avon Books, 1981.

★Can be ordered from Alzheimer's Disease Association (Connecticut chapter: 203-288-0214).

About the Authors

Dr. Alan Siegal is director of the Center for Geriatric and Adult Psychiatry Inc. in Hamden, Connecticut, a multi-disciplinary group practice specializing in geriatric care. In addition to his clinical practice, he is medical director of the Alzheimer Resource Center of Connecticut, a 120-bed skilled nursing facility dedicated to the care of Alzheimer patients. Dr. Siegal is also the president of the American Association for Geriatric Psychiatry. He received his training in psychiatry and geriatric psychiatry at Yale University School of Medicine.

Robert S. Siegal is currently the Director of Original Programming for USA Networks, with more than fifteen years experience writing and producing for film and television. He is a Magna Cum Laude graduate from Adelphi University with a B.A. in Communications. Siegal lives on the New Jersey shore with his wife Robin and their four children. *Forget Me Not* is his first book.

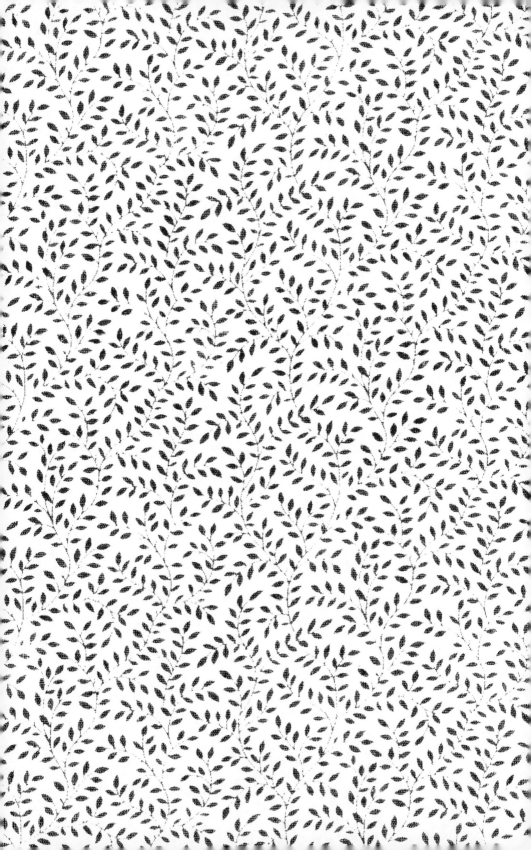